RULE & REIGN

The Faith-Walker Manual

JULIANA PAGE

BALBOA.PRESS

A DIVISION OF HAY HOUSE

Balboa Press books may be ordered through booksellers or by contacting:

Balboa Press
A Division of Hay House
1663 Liberty Drive
Bloomington, IN 47403
www.balboapress.com
844-682-1282

Because of the dynamic nature of the Internet, any web addresses or links contained in this book may have changed since publication and may no longer be valid. The views expressed in this work are solely those of the author and do not necessarily reflect the views of the publisher, and the publisher hereby disclaims any responsibility for them.

The author of this book does not dispense medical advice or prescribe the use of any technique as a form of treatment for physical, emotional, or medical problems without the advice of a physician, either directly or indirectly. The intent of the author is only to offer information of a general nature to help you in your quest for emotional and spiritual well-being. In the event you use any of the information in this book for yourself, which is your constitutional right, the author and the publisher assume no responsibility for your actions.

Any people depicted in stock imagery provided by Getty Images are models, and such images are being used for illustrative purposes only.
Certain stock imagery © Getty Images.

Unless otherwise noted, all scripture quotations are from the Holy Bible, New International Version. Copyright 1973, 1978, 1984, 2011 by Biblica, Inc. Used by permission. All rights reserved worldwide.

Scripture quotations marked (AMP) are from the Amplified Bible. Copyright 2015 by The Lockman Foundation, La Habra, CA 90631. Used by permission. All rights reserved. Any italics occur in the original.

Scripture quotations marked (ESV) are from The Holy Bible, English Standard Version. Text Edition: 2016. Copyright 2001 by Crossway Bibles, a publishing ministry of Good News Publishers. Used by permission. All rights reserved.

Scripture quotations marked (KJV) are from the King James Version of the Bible (public domain).

Scripture quotations marked (NASB) are from the New American Standard Bible, Copyright 1960, 1971, 1977, 1995 by The Lockman Foundation. All rights reserved.

Scripture quotations marked (NCV) are from The Holy Bible, New Century Version. Copyright 2005 by Thomas Nelson, Inc. Used by permission. All rights reserved.

Scripture quotations marked (NKJV) are from the New King James Version. Copyright 1982 by Thomas Nelson. Used by permission. All rights reserved.

Scripture quotations marked (NLT) are from the Holy Bible, New Living Translation. Copyright 1996, 2004, 2015 by Tyndale House Foundation. Used by permission of Tyndale House Publishers, Inc., Carol Stream, Illinois 60188. All rights reserved.

Scripture quotations marked (TPT) are from The Passion Translation. Copyright 2017, 2018, 2020 by Passion & Fire Ministries, Inc. Used by permission. All rights reserved. thePassionTranslation.com

Scripture quotations marked (YLT) from Young's Literal Translation of the Bible (public domain).

ISBN: 978-1-9822-7143-5 (sc)
ISBN: 978-1-9822-7144-2 (e)

Print information available on the last page.

Balboa Press rev. date: 07/13/2021

CONTENTS

Introduction

Activate Kingdom Influence & Actualize Your Potential

Enter by the narrow gate. For the gate is wide and the way is easy that leads
to destruction, and those who enter by it are many. For the gate is narrow
and the way is hard that leads to life, and those who find it are few.

—Matthew 7:13-14 ESV

What does it look like to have the abundant life that Jesus preached about? Perhaps you've
wrestled with this. Maybe you've tried dying to yourself and performing but it only led to burnout.
Maybe you were diligent about going to church and serving but you never experienced real life
change and resented going through the motions. If you've simply felt like something is missing
in your life and you haven't been able to crack the code, you can learn something new. You can
learn how to live as a partaker of the divine nature of God and experience the fulfilment that
comes from awakening to His true nature as it's revealed in and through you. Could it be that
this is what you've been missing or waiting for? For the creation waits in eager expectation for
the children of God to be revealed" (Romans 8:19 NIV).

Jesus did not die on the cross so that we might die, but so that we may live, activate our
influence, and actualize our full potential. "The thief comes only to steal and kill and destroy; I
have come that they may have life, and have it to the full" (John 10:10)! In other words, we can
discover what a resurrected lifestyle looks like, and then passionately pursue that supernatural
way of life. Believing that these things are available and determining to find the keys for releasing
them are both vital for anyone who wants to experience everything that Jesus gave us through
His death and resurrection.

The believer's journey is not of learning and doing; it's a lifelong, interactive relationship with
God. It's how we're radically transformed through supernatural experiences and encounters with
God's love, God's Word and with the Holy Spirit. What does it mean to live from the Presence
of the Holy Spirit who has made you His dwelling place? It means that we can live under the
influence of God every day! That's how we're designed to live. We are designed to grow and
mature in Christ, however, when discipleship and spiritual development are absent from a vibrant
lifestyle of Holy Spirit encounters, we're left starved. Information alone cannot fill our hunger
and constant activity can't fill our thirst.

What sets us apart as the people of God? What sets us apart is the One who lives within us. A journey with God of ruling and reigning on earth is not about information or activity; it's about living from the Presence of the One who has made you His dwelling place. Get ready for increased hope and practical keys for personal victory. Prepare yourself for a gift of faith that will release the supernatural in you and through you like never before. This is an activating manual. As you read and practice these spiritual gold nuggets, may you be transformed by the revelation of our good and empowering God who is calling all His children into an abundant and fruitful life.

Remember: this is a resource for you. Interact with it honestly. Fill the blank pages and journal spaces with your thoughts, impressions, and interactions with the Holy Spirit. Consider it a vehicle to help you experience the Presence of God in a whole new dimension.

The curriculum can be done as a small group, a class or an individual experience. You would first read the section and then work through the appropriate manual exercises throughout the week. The schedule would involve you working through one session and its interactive activations and exercises each week. If the activations are being done in a group or class setting, the group leader can set aside an appropriate amount of time at the end of the class for those that want to share their experiences. This is where the information learned in each section will be processed and implemented.

For the question prompts and activations, you can answer and work through these in the space provided or in a separate notebook. It's recommended that you personally work through each of the exercises on your own time so that you can fully process the concepts you are learning. Feel free to celebrate your journey of living under the active and continuous influence of the Spirit of God with the Rule and Reign Manual using these hashtags on social media: **#godsvibesmatter** and **#ruleandreign**

Lord, heighten my spiritual senses to
see that which is not visible
hear that which is not audible
sense that which is not tangible
believe that which is unbelievable.

Teach me to sort through
The noises of this world to
hear and discern Your powerful,
wonderful, pure, precious voice.

GOD'S VIBES MATTER.
Feel His Presence. Hear His Voice. Experience and Release His Power.

Part One

WAKE-UP, SLEEPER

This is why it is said: Wake up, sleeper, rise from
the dead, and Christ will shine on you.

—Ephesians 5:14 NIV

When you think of receiving a gift, what comes to mind? More than likely, the first thing that came to your mind was not hitting rock bottom. Rock bottom is hard, terrifying even, but if we embrace it, it's also a gift. Rock bottom shakes us up and wakes us up from the things that simply don't work anymore. When we hit rock bottom or the bottom of the level we're currently on, (yes, we'll have many bottoms and peel back many layers on our growth journeys) essentially our masks, roles, patterns, means of control, and ego don't work anymore, and we can't keep all that up. That's the gift.

We don't have a to stay in pain and suffering, we can grow. A lot of us have never learned how to turn our pain into something more peaceful and powerful. Many of us live in pain internally most of our lives without others even knowing about it. We can, however, turn our pain into power, embrace our truth and live free. If we don't, we pass on pain, powerless patterns and cause more harm than good to ourselves and others. We can repress pain if we decide to, but that never gets rid of it. Ultimately, something must give and it's an opportunity for us to enter a portal of new awakening and higher consciousness.

When we choose to arise and shine from the bottom, the freedom, strength, and power we can operate in can make us question why we ever settled for anything less. When we choose to embrace rock bottom, we also get to choose the path to sovereignty where we take radical responsibility for our healing and thus shift from being disempowered to empowered. We can't navigate this in our own strength and understanding, so it's important to have Holy Spirit and a coach or a therapist actively involved on the journey.

God wants us to heal and mature. He releases revelation in the season it is needed, but He confounds the lists, strategies, and formulas we create. It's often our rock bottoms that lead us to seek answers and tools not found in previous modalities we've researched or trained in. We can't substitute head knowledge for an active relationship with the Holy Spirit. As believers in Christ, filled with the Holy Spirit, we have access to the clearest, most direct pathway to truth and the power of God. The Holy Spirit reveals truth to our spirit and soul if we will spend our life seeking to know Him deeply and intimately.

You may worry about your future and be afraid to change and if you decide to walk humbly with God, you'll discover that His perfect love casts out all fear. We all worry about things that we don't have any control over and don't have the power to change. All worrying, however, is a lack of trust in God. Transformation begins when we stop hiding and pretending and start trusting and walking intimately with God. You may have been in a role, a habit, or a hang-up for so long that it has become your identity. You may be thinking, what will happen if I really commit to inner healing? Will I change? If I give up my old ways of being, habits and unhealthy outlets, what will I become? Who or what will I lose? Who will I be? Because of our fear of the unknown or because of our despair, we may close our minds because we don't think we deserve any better. Know upfront that before you can make any progress on your journey, you need to face your unworthiness. Any unworthiness is denial, it's denying your true self from operating freely.

Whenever we choose to deny what we know, we create a false system of beliefs to keep us from honestly looking in the mirror and facing the truth. As children we learn various coping skills and self-protecting roles and behaviors to keep us safe. As the years progress, these roles can dominate our lives and cloud our view. When we live in denial, we disable our feelings, lose energy, short-circuit our growth, isolate ourselves from God, alienate ourselves from relationships and prolong pain. When we instead choose the path to rule and reign in life, we invest in our conscious evolution; meaning we no longer accept sleep walking through life.

I remember being faced with the excruciating weight of not knowing how to answer a few key questions: *Who am I? Why am I here? What is my life meant for?* I was a freshman in college standing in a career services office staring at a flyer that said, "Know Thyself Retreat." Prior to this, I was an athlete, I was an honor student, I was a reliable people pleaser and co-dependent in my family system, and I was a rule follower that was just chugging along, checking off the lists I was conditioned to check off to avoid pain and suffering at all costs. Without the people-pleasing, the co-dependency, and the roles, I felt completely unprepared for the future and the questions kept me up at night. The ways that I was pretending and unconsciously inauthentic, didn't work anymore. I was totally freaked out because I couldn't recognize that this was my portal into the wonderful new where I was finally without my defenses. It was an opportunity to go deep to figure out who I am with God and without all the roles and labels.

I'd love to tell you that I went to that retreat and hope was restored and my life was turned around for the better, but that's not what happened. While I did go to the retreat, my inner life was too loud to fully embrace the journal prompts, nature walks and guided exercises. It would take roughly eleven more years of searching to answer these questions and discover my personal path to power until I finally stopped the search once and for all to seek the Source. While I took many risks and stacked many accomplishments, what I eventually had to come to was what I'd been running from all along; I didn't know how to have and enjoy my life, how to steward it well or serve in a way that didn't leave me burned out and bitter. I didn't want to run my life anymore and yet I was terrified not to, but I desperately needed divine guidance and I was determined to find it.

Waking-up to our greatness is scary. It requires accepting that we have lived under the influence of who we thought we should or had to be and buried our greatness. It also requires changing our standards and making necessary adjustments to pursue the highest expression of our truth. Many of us have greatness but that doesn't mean we can handle it. We may know we have greatness in our hands and yet we don't know how to steward it. Greatness has guidelines and it needs guidance. All of us need somebody to see our blind spots to pull the greatness out of us.

One of the worst mistakes we can make on our evolving journey it to allow arrogance to block the guidance that will take our greatness to the next level. We can be so full of pride to think that we've got it and we've got our lives figured out that we miss the guidance that will cultivate and hone our greatness. Arrogance will always intercept the guidance that we need. Humility is the definition of greatness. We are not actually great until we know how much we need God and how incomplete we are without Him. Freedom comes when we realize Who is most significant in our lives. Jesus demonstrates this in His Sermon on the Mount, beginning His sermon not with commandments, but with promises of God's blessing on heart attitudes. He began focusing on the heart, doing heart surgery, wanting to reconstruct our hearts and bring our hearts in tune with his. The Beatitudes describe the foundational character qualities and family characteristics Jesus wanted to be at work in his people.

The paradox of the Kingdom of God is that letting go is getting everything. We let go of our ambitions, ideas, ways, theories, and attachments. There is nothing wrong with these or desiring to be everything that God has called us to be, God just wants to check our motives for greatness. He wants us to ask Him to help us be humble where we can walk in the totality of our greatness. We see this exemplified in the gospel of Mark. "People were bringing little children to Jesus for him to place his hands on them, but the disciples rebuked them. When Jesus saw this, he was indignant. He said to them, "Let the little children come to me, and do not hinder them, for the kingdom of God belongs to such as these. Truly I tell you, anyone who will not receive the kingdom of God like a little child will never enter it." And he took the children in his arms, placed his hands on them and blessed them" (Mark 10:13-16). To really be able to relate with and trust God, we are to become like children in our eagerness and pursuit of relationship with Him.

Living in victim consciousness with an orphan spirit is where we get stuck. Not healing and not moving on are ways we remain victims. When we blame others for taking our power away, we give them our power. True empowerment is to take all power back. Sleeping (remaining unconscious) and surviving don't require conscious choices.

Challenging and healing frightened parts of ourselves requires conscious choices, and we cannot grow spiritually without challenging and healing them. The changes we create in ourselves are the changes we create in the world. The journey to rule and reign is one that we were born to take. Only you can decide when to begin it, and only you can do the work to complete it, but it's not a journey that you can travel in your own strength and understanding.

The journey to fulfil your potential will be long, difficult, and frightening, and only you can make it. It will also be exhilarating, fulfilling and your return on investment for the life God has given you. To rule and reign, we pursue our destiny as kings and queens by taking responsibility for our experiences and using them to learn about ourselves. We're whole new beings learning how to be new beings. In prophetic times of growth, where the Lord is looking to accelerate us, promote us and elevate us from our current positions to where He needs us to be according to the plan that He has for our lives, God will make sure we are in the right places at the right times and that we get the tools, edification, course corrections, strategic instruction, and the Word that we need. Perhaps this is a divine appointment for you.

Activation: We discover our destiny as we commit to our relationship with God. It's through relationship where we share His hope as we discover who God made us to be. We find our identity in Him and grow in Him and His heart attitudes by implementing His Beatitudes. We learn that God's grace and power are often revealed in weaknesses, and the most important thing any believer can do is decide to believe in Jesus. Jesus sees us through a developed lens of love. It was the Father's point of view. He sees us as we are; the restored, original, intentional version of God's heart.

Consider the following Beatitudes and blessings Jesus shares in Matthew 5:3-12:

"Blessed are the poor in spirit"
- *the foundation for a relationship with God*
- losing hope in yourself and finding your only hope in God.

"Blessed are those who mourn"
- *the foundation for repentance*
- seeing the true grievousness of sin.

"Blessed are the meek"
- *the foundation for faith*
- quieting your soul to trust God in all circumstances.

"Blessed are those who hunger and thirst for righteousness"
- *the foundation for living and sanctification*
- the pursuit of holiness in your life and in the world.

"Blessed are the merciful"
- *the foundation for relationships*
- loving others as God has loved us.

"Blessed are the pure in heart"
- *the foundation for worship*
- having a vision of God 'win out' over all other things.

"Blessed are the peacemakers"
- *the foundation for mission*
- seeking to bring God's offer of peace to a hostile world.

"Blessed are the persecuted"
- *the foundation for perseverance*
- knowing and following our Savior through many tribulations for the joy set before us.

Which one of the Beatitudes resonates with you the most, and why?

Which do you think is better, reliance on self-power or reliance on God's power? Why?

What practical application will you apply to help you live out the Beatitudes in your life?

Write this down in a journal and say it aloud with conviction and intention:

I AM READY, OPEN AND WILLING TO SEE THINGS DIFFERNTLY.

I AM NOW WILLING TO HAVE A SHIFT IN MY
PERCEPTION OF GOD AND AROUND ANY OTHER
AREA IN NEED OF TRASNFORMATION.

I AM AVAILABLE TO SEE PATTERNS, CLOSE DOORS,
REARRANGE PARADIGMS, AND ENTER INTO THE
WONDERFUL NEW LIFE I'VE BEEN GIVEN.

This week: Notice any area(s) where you have been playing a role, living a lie or just going through the motions. What are you being led to release (what simply isn't working anymore) to create more space for your relationship with God and for His power to manifest in your life? Get alone with God, no distractions. Cast these cares from your heart onto Him and ask Him to show up strong in your weaknesses.

KNOW YOUR WORTH

I praise you, for I am fearfully and wonderfully made.
Wonderful are your works; my soul knows it very well.

—Psalm 139:14 ESV

The formation of our identity is one of the most important conflicts that we face. Often, those that struggle with an identity crisis are persuaded to fix the crisis by looking inward to explore and ask questions about what makes them happy and what doesn't. Unfortunately, any time we look within without God, we become more confused and depressed. When it comes to identity, we can discover the supernatural peace that surpasses all understanding when we settle our soul's deepest question with God first and keep Him intimately involved in our becoming.

Ignorance is not bliss when it comes to our becoming, it's catastrophic especially when we're ignorant of ourselves and who we really are. When we live disconnected from God, from His Word and from the influence of the Holy Spirit, we step out from His covering and protection. The prophet Hosea warned the people of Israel about this, "My people are destroyed for lack of knowledge [of My law, where I reveal My will]. Because you [the priestly nation] have rejected knowledge, I will also reject you from being My priest. Since you have forgotten the law of your God, I will also forget your children" (Hosea 4:6 AMP). Notice this verse doesn't say sinners are destroyed for lack of knowledge. It says God's people are destroyed because of their lack of knowledge. This infers that if God's people had knowledge of who they really are in Christ, of who God is, and of the rights and privileges of their dominion—they wouldn't be destroyed. One reason Satan is often able to reign, or rule, in the life of believers is because those believers do not realize the authority that has been given to them.

When we get a spiritual apprehension of our seat at the right hand of the Father, things will change because we will change them; we will take authority over the things that are under the curse. We understand how to do this through spiritual enlightenment. The authority that we have as believers comes by revelation. As we embrace our authority, we can more plainly see our role in establishing God's kingdom on earth. God is the head; we're the body and the head needs the body to bring His will to pass on earth. The Apostle Paul championed this teaching in his epistle to the Ephesians:

[I always pray] that the God of our Lord Jesus Christ, the Father of glory, may grant you a spirit of wisdom and of revelation [that gives you a deep and personal and intimate insight] into the true knowledge of Him [for we know the Father through the Son]. And [I pray] that the eyes of your heart [the very center and core of your being] may be enlightened [flooded with light by the Holy Spirit], so that you will know *and* cherish the hope [the divine guarantee, the confident expectation] to which He has called you, the riches of His glorious inheritance in the saints (God's people), and [so that you will begin to know] what the immeasurable *and* unlimited *and* surpassing greatness of His [active, spiritual] power is in us who believe. These are in accordance with the working of His mighty strength which He produced in Christ when He raised Him from the dead and seated Him at His own right hand in the heavenly *places*, far above all rule and authority and power and dominion [whether angelic or human], and [far above] every name that is named [above every title that can be conferred], not only in this age *and* world but also in the one to come (Ephesians 1:17-21).

God loves us and His Word is designed to fuel our beings and gives us truth that helps us to align with His highest good. Anything that is unresolved in our lives can greatly affect how our lives look. When we recognize that we are not orphans or slaves but royalty and sons and daughters, we have different expectations regarding our lives, we focus and give energy to different things and we think differently about our lives.

When we know who we are as sons, we walk differently than those trying to earn God's love and acceptance. Some have a spiritual inferiority complex because they haven't received this revelation—we're not orphaned creatures, we're a new creatures! Second Corinthians 5:17 says, "Therefore if any man be in Christ, he is a new creature: old things are passed away; behold, all things are become new." God doesn't make any unrighteous new creatures. We have been made the righteousness of God in Christ Jesus (2 Corinthians 5:21 KJV). This means that we're not working to be righteous, we're working to remove anything that keeps us from knowing that we are and learning to mature in reigning and comprehending and expressing our righteousness.

Many times, believers think Jesus is going to do everything for them in this process; they do not realize they have a part to play. Notice that Romans 5:17 doesn't say, "Jesus Christ will reign through you." No! It says, "...THEY [that's us] which receive abundance of grace and of the gift of righteousness shall reign in life by one, Jesus Christ." This verse says that you and I will reign. Of course, it's by, or because of, Jesus Christ that we have this authority, but He has given us the authority to rule and reign.

Some say, "I've left it up to the Lord; He's going to do it." But, no, the truth is, He has left it up to us! It's on us to discover our worth, tap into our power and own our position. Romans 5:17 mentions two things we have received: abundance of grace and the gift of righteousness. It's receiving the abundance of grace and the gift of righteousness that enables us to reign. If we don't know what we've received, we'll be hindered in reigning. It's imperative to know that we are made alive in Christ. The Apostle Paul encourages the Ephesians again about what they and we have an opportunity to awaken to:

> and [so that you will begin to know] what the immeasurable *and* unlimited *and* surpassing greatness of His [active, spiritual] power is in us who believe. These are in accordance with the working of His mighty strength which He produced in Christ when He raised Him from the dead and seated Him at His own right hand in the heavenly *places*, far above all rule and authority and power and dominion [whether angelic or human], and [far above] every name that is named [above every title that can be conferred], not only in this age *and* world but also in the one to come. And He put all things [in every realm] in subjection under Christ's feet, and appointed Him as [supreme and authoritative] head over all things in the church, which is His body, the fullness of Him who fills *and* completes all things in all [believers] (Ephesians 1:19-2-6 AMP).

When we don't see ourselves fully, we settle for inferior things. "For whoever lacks these *qualities* is blind—shortsighted [closing his spiritual eyes to the truth], having become oblivious to the fact that he was cleansed from his old sins" (2 Peter 1:9). These blind spots always lead to brokenness and broken consciousness. We're born to rule, but we're trained to settle. As children, we should have been protected and educated, but when that doesn't happen, we learn the tough lessons of life through experiences rather than the safe instruction of paternal voices. There is a need to make sure that the foundation of our worth is settled in the right place because the world intentionally breaks our souls. We can be miseducated to function as slaves rather than as royalty when we're naive and ignorant as to how to move and operate in the world.

As we live, there are so many different things that come to make us question our worth. We go through loss, divorce, failure, so many things that make us question our value. The world determines our value by what we have and what we do. God determines our value by who we are and who we "be" versus what we "do." God measures worth by our being not our doing. All healthy doing comes from healthy being. If we can be worthy and sit in our worthiness and find the courage to agree with God's view of us, we can live in greater freedom and wholeness and unlock this for others. The more you voluntarily love what God loves, the more life-giving, free and satisfying your relationship is with Him because you will become rooted in the place of trusting Him constantly to work out His plans in your life.

When we take our question of worth to the world, be it something we find our identity in (relationship, job, role, image), what happens when that thing falls apart? What happens when the very thing that our whole identity was anchored in goes away? Whatever we place our worth and our value in that's outside of us, it puts us in a fragile position and if that thing changes, then we lose our sense of anchoring in who we are. When we take our question of worth to the world, we allow other people who may still be struggling with their own worth and their own sense of identity to tell us who we are. We also are susceptible to outside things defining and informing us instead of allowing the Spirit of God to settle us.

Worthiness is something that must be settled with God from the inside out. We can ask Him to give us a revelation of who we are in Him. Then and only then, we won't go to the world and ask, *"am I worthy,"* but we will show up in the the world and say, *"I am worthy."* We don't take our question of worth to the world; we take our answer which is our worth and worthiness. We learn this deeply and intimately as we spend time with God. When we sit and we cultivate our soul, we understand that God settled our worth. He isn't questioning His creation and what He formed before we entered the world. He delights in us. When Jeremiah wrestled with his worth, God encouraged him, "Before I formed you in the womb I knew you, before you were born I set you apart; I appointed you as a prophet to the nations" (Jeremiah 1:5 KJV).

Whether we have a hard time believing it or not, God doesn't change our price. When we believe we're worthy, we go out, we create, and we walk worthy of the calling on our lives. Once we see our value, our lives get so much easier because we stop putting the pressure and the expectation and the burden on people and things outside of us and we embrace the truth of who we are. When we stop hustling and driving to prove our worth, we can sit and rest in our worth and when we rest in our worth, we take our answers to the world instead of our questions.

One of the divine encounters that was pivotal in settling my worth happened unexpectantly. It was an encounter I didn't know I needed and wouldn't have known to ask for. While I was serving during a church conference, I was able to catch the tail end of a sermon where a guest speaker was guiding the attendees through an activation. The activation was to ask God what your name is, who is He calling you. As I looked around the auditorium, women were sharing things like chosen, beautiful, worthy, daughter, and free. All I heard was silence.

The activation was new to me. I didn't even consider that I could ask God a question like that or that He'd answer. As I witnessed women experiencing shifts, something stirred in me and I was eager to get with God in my quiet time where He had my full attention, and I could receive my answer. I didn't find it random that I caught that piece of the conference or that I didn't hear anything. I chose to see it as a teaser for what God wanted to reveal to me.

Over the next few weeks, I still didn't receive my name, but things we're culminating. I'd been writing my very first book in that season and I'd received an email from the publisher advising me to consider a few options before publishing. Initially, I felt discouraged because this seemed like a hindrance to bringing the book into the world, but as I sat with the email, I felt inspired to move forward using a pen name, something I'd never considered. Sensing a correlation with a new name, literally, I brought this before the Lord and asked again for my new name. I waited for a response and found myself doodling Juliana Page in cursive in my notebook. After writing it a few times, I was inspired to reach out to Google for name meanings for each name and found that Juliana meant youthful or joyful and Page meant servant or messenger. Immediately, I felt a resonance in my spirit, that was exactly who I am, a youthful servant and a joyful messenger.

Feeling relieved, but wanting to be sure, I gave myself some time to respond to the publisher and asked God to confirm this to me in a way I couldn't miss and would understand. The same afternoon, I walked into a leadership meeting and the pastor said *"Hey, Juliana"* on "accident" as I entered her office. She apologized and admitted she didn't know why she'd said that, but all I could do was smile because I knew exactly where the prophetic slip had come from and received it as my confirmation.

What I love most about how God gave me a new name, was how it shifted my narrative and was a constant self-check of who I am being in the world. I am adopted in the natural and this felt like a redeeming affirmation of my adoption into God's royal family. I no longer had to question who I was or what I should be doing, just purposely live out who God called me one day at a time and one moment at a time. It felt like a weight was lifted and I could finally just be and enjoy becoming the fullness of who I was becoming.

Who we are being in the world is based on our level of conscious awareness of who we believe we are. This determines what and who we are going to attract and what type of life we will live. It's how we create our world. Partnering with God is a relationship that unlocks our unlimited potential. It's through connecting with Him and being willing to obey His promptings that we're able to raise our consciousness to achieve new levels of understanding and carrying capacity of His anointing so that we can enjoy more freedom in every aspect of our lives.

Trust with God is courageously built. We are the only ones, with the power of the Holy Spirit can transform ourselves from being disempowered people to empowered people. We can make different healthy and life-giving choices instead of unhealthy ones like overeating, smoking, watching pornography, shopping, gambling, drinking alcohol, using drugs, or having mindless sex. We can choose our emotions, including the most painful, to grow spiritually instead of wrestling with obsessive thoughts, compulsive actions, and addictive behaviors. We can choose to experience uncomfortable states (overwhelm, stress, inadequacy, resentment) and challenge the frightened part of ourselves to respond instead of reacting. When we are self-aware and our hearts are pure, we can see God in others. When unconditional love flows from our hearts, we move through life and engage with others with compassion.

It can take a while to shed our old conditioning. The difference between being a slave or orphan (living as an orphan rather than a child of God) and royal is consciousness. Lack of self-awareness causes us to settle for standards that are beneath us because of an empty self-esteem. When we're chained, we become incapable of embracing the future. Our authentic self is the energy and frequency of the Holy Spirit, that gives life and supernatural power. Our old nature is any negative self-talk, any limiting narrative, and any form of beating ourselves up from within. As we become adept at recognizing these and taking any thought captive that exults itself above the truth, we change our insides.

We are great creators because we are made in the image of the Creator. When we renew our self-concept or who we believe we are, by embracing our identity in Christ, everything else shifts as well; what we do and how we do it. We can break out of any box by God's power and for His glory. While we think we're going to change the world for God, He changes us for the world. Holy Spirit helps keep us accountable to the truth and empower us to represent God well.

Before we deconstruct and rebuild the world around us, starting with ourselves, we need a greater understanding of God's intention and what's blocked us from it. The Bible tells us that God is light and we are made in His image and likeness; we are the light of the world. Our natural mind has a hard time wrapping itself around this idea. We are largely unaware of and influenced by our surroundings and subconsciously imprinted by our world. Physically we can't act as light does, but by faith we can live and operate like God as we fine tune our frequency or vibe (comprised of our beliefs, thoughts, feelings, emotions, words, the condition of our hearts and actions) to align with Him. God gave me a phrase for this, *"God's Vibes Matter."* We're aware of what vibes and energy but not all vibes matter or are worth partnering with and giving airtime too. God's vibes, His character, His Presence, His power, His will and His heart are what I was being called to align with, so this phrase is a constant reminder to pay attention to what I'm partnering with and giving life to.

We are always sowing seeds and whatever we sow we will reap a harvest of. When we are operating out of our own strength and understanding, often we fall out of line with God's Heart and His Word. As we seek the kingdom first and actively pursue righteousness, peace, and joy, we increase our faith and shift our frequency. When we open ourselves up to God and pay attention to His Presence, not only does He satisfy our needs and the longings of our heart, but He also helps us live healthy and whole lives and guides us to manifest a kingdom destiny that bears much fruit.

Here are a few examples of what activating God's vibes looks like:

1. Seeking His Kingdom first in place of seeking things of the world
2. Being filled with the Holy Spirit (letting our cup overflow) instead of giving into carnality
3. Edifying, building up, comforting, and encouraging one another rather than judging and criticizing
4. Worshiping the Lord in our hearts and keeping our hearts pure before Him
5. Living in a state of gratitude and humility to the Lord

Living these out will radically shift our vibe and empower us to abide in a state of peace and joy no matter what we're facing or what we encounter. God empowers us to work on our focus because it's how we transform and become, and it also impacts our body, soul, and spirit. This requires diligent and deliberate seeking. What holds us back and keeps us asleep is our broken consciousness:

- Our past experiences
- Our inherited beliefs
- Memories we develop before age 3-4 (when chronological memory begins)
- Our trapped emotions and inner child wounds
- Beliefs that are formed from billions of experiences that we give meaning to
- Generational emotions and beliefs handed down
- Father wounds that can become an obsession in adulthood
- False concepts of beauty, image, and status
- Toxic relationships

Reclaiming who we really are is a process; nothing changes if nothing changes. When we reclaim ourselves, we know how to stay grounded in our authentic selves regardless of what's happening around us. It's no longer about who we attach to that brings our value but connecting with God and expressing compassion and our authentic self. When we cultivate this awareness, we realize quickly when we are acting ways that aren't helpful to ourselves or others and can spot those situations when we are feeding our carnal nature instead of living in peace. Knowing our worth is about maintaining awareness of God, our anchor while engaging with the world, remembering that we're in the world but not of it. It's a spiritual discipline that requires self-control to free our minds of our own thinking and being affected by the projections of others. We can't give to others what we don't have for ourselves. We can begin opening up to unconditional love for ourselves and uncovering our worth by:

1. Releasing bitter roots
2. Making space for the wonderful new and transformation/new beliefs
3. Tuning ourselves to God's frequency with His Word and keys that deliberately reprogram subconscious beliefs and ultimately our lifestyle (meditating on the Word visualizing His Promises, Prophetic soaking)

The question of our worth is one that we take to God. God how do you see me? What do you say I am? What's your view of me? One of the most challenging things you can do is ask God these questions and then sit and let your soul receive the revolution of that answer. Revelation moments really open us up to greater capacity. God can be the most relatable person in our lives if we allow Him to be. He can become the answer to all our questions and enable us to grow and expand in ways that are greater than we can think or imagine.

Sometimes we can even sit with God and ask Him for the name He gave us because God named us before we were even formed in our mother's womb. God typically in Scripture will change the name of someone when He changes their identity, sense of worth and the value that they see about themselves. Names carry a powerful vibration and weight and embracing them is a cultivation of the soul.

> *Activation:* Who we are affects what we do and how we do it. Our awareness of who we really are, as opposed to the who we believe we are and that we were taught that we are can be quite different. This exercise is to help you become more aware of who God says you are, what He tells you to do and how He inspires you to do it.
>
> Ask God to give you a new name. What did He have in mind when He created you? Press in for Him to give you a revelation of you; the God-revealed self you're becoming. In the circles below or in a notebook, make a list in each circle of who God says you are, what He leads you to do, and how He inspires you to do it. When you're tuned in to His frequency, there isn't any resistance and you're flowing in the kingdom, righteousness, peace, and joy.

Catching a Vision

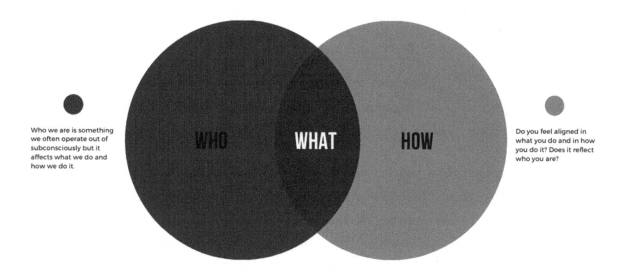

Who we are is something we often operate out of subconsciously but it affects what we do and how we do it.

WHO **WHAT** **HOW**

Do you feel aligned in what you do and in how you do it? Does it reflect who you are?

This week: Fine tune your frequency and let your light shine.

Look at yourself in the mirror and notice all the self-judgements that arise in the next few moments. Take a moment to listen to those judgements. Your emotions will let you know which ones affect you the most, as the stronger the negative feeling, the more attached you are to the judgement. Write the judgement that incites the strongest emotional response on a piece of paper. Underneath the judgement, write down the answers to the following questions:

Is this judgement you learned from someone else? Can you remember when you learned it and from whom?

Have you repeated this judgement about yourself to someone else?

How has this judgement shaped your actions? Have you denied yourself opportunities or failed to take risks because of it?

Does this judgement match with who God says you are? Do you still want to let this judgement control your life?

If the answer is yes to the last question, that's fine if it's truly what you want. Perhaps you will come back to this at a later point to find that you no longer need this belief. If you answered no to the last question, now, the time has come to let this go and the first step is to forgive yourself for using it against you.

When you are ready to release this judgement, say the following statement out loud:

> *"I _____, have used my negative self-talk to subjugate myself with conditional love. I forgive myself for doing so and I will now let this false belief go. God says I am _____, and I fully align with this now.*

Every time you find yourself falling back into self-judgement on this issue, repeat this statement of forgiveness again. Doing so is an act of bringing God's unconditional love to yourself. He already paid the price for your self-judgement; you don't need to do so anymore. Through self-forgiveness you can walk in your worth and the newness of life God offers.

GET YOUR FIGHT BACK

Practice these things, immerse yourself in them,
so that all may see your progress.

—1 Timothy 4:15 ESV

*I*t is unnatural for growth not to take place in anything that God has created. Growth is natural but it requires that we are intentional about leaning into and sustaining the growth that is attached to our lives. Healthy things grow, evolve, and constantly improve. If you're not growing and evolving something is wrong. Something has disrupted the natural divine order of things. There is dis-ease somewhere.

If we ever wondered where to find wisdom for our personal growth journey, the book of Proverbs is chock-full of wisdom to for reigning in life. Here are a few gems from Proverbs 16:

The plans *and* reflections of the heart belong to man, but the [wise] answer of the tongue is from the Lord. All the ways of a man are clean *and* innocent in his own eyes [and he may see nothing wrong with his actions], but the Lord weighs *and* examines the motives *and* intents [of the heart and knows the truth]. Commit your works to the Lord [submit and trust them to Him], and your plans will succeed [if you respond to His will and guidance] (Proverbs 16:1-3 AMP).

A man's mind plans his way [as he journeys through life], but the Lord directs his steps *and* establishes them (Proverbs 16:9).

He who pays attention to the word [of God] will find good, and blessed (happy, prosperous, to be admired) is he who trusts [confidently] in the Lord. The wise in heart will be called understanding, and sweet speech increases persuasiveness *and* learning [in both speaker and listener]. Understanding (spiritual insight) is a [refreshing and boundless] wellspring of life to those who have it (Proverbs 16:19-22).

Kings detest wrongdoing, for a throne is established through righteousness (Proverbs 16:12 NIV).

Whoever is slow to anger is better than the mighty, and he who rules his spirit than he who takes a city (Proverbs 16:32 ESV).

Meditating (meaning to mull over in our minds or to think through) on this chapter in the book of Proverbs a few things stand out:

- God cares about our insides—the motives and intent of our hearts
- When we humble ourselves and turn our plans and work over to Him, He will help us align with His will and cause our plans to succeed
- We can plan our path all we want (self-help, force, push, figure out) but God guides and establishes our steps
- When we pay attention to God's Word we grow in confidence and understanding and become a wellspring of life for others
- Ruling and reigning is established through righteousness (not unworthiness, insecurity, doubt, or unbelief)
- Ruling our spirit and exercising self-control over our inner life makes us powerful

In just one chapter of one book of the Bible we find several instances of how to grow, rule and reign in life. While walking out the depth of these verses requires the help of the Holy Spirit, we don't have to overthink the process or make it any more complicated than it is written. We are transformed by the renewing of our mind. As we read God's Word, contemplate, and reflect on it, pay attention to what's being highlighted to us or resonating with our spirit and obey as opportunities are presented (and they will be), we grow and mature in Christ and our Christlikeness. A simple growth formula could be:

1. Make space for consistent, quality time with God daily
2. Study God's Word, meditate on it, and journal wisdom points
3. Pray for strength, wisdom, awareness, and self-control to walk out new levels of understanding by God's power and for His glory

Investing in our relationship doesn't have to be complicated. It's usually the small, consistent sacrifices that add up and build us up. As we invest, we are purified, refreshed, strengthened, and developed to shine brighter and brighter. Faith comes by hearing, but specifically by hearing the Word of God. We can't expect to grow and mature in Christ if we don't receive and know His Word. God supplies what we need, but it does require our whole-hearted commitment and investment to do life with Him.

Commitment sounds like a good idea but following through is where the harvest is. Unfortunately, loss almost always has an impact on our belief. Loss chips at our belief slowly and sometimes it happens unconsciously, and there's nothing that stifles growth quite like unbelief. We often don't recognize we're not growing until what used to work doesn't anymore. When we can't function the way, we're designed to, our faith has been chipped away at for some time and there is a disease called unbelief that is robbing us of our fight.

Do a quick self-check:

Has your belief been quarantined in a season of consecutive losses?

Do you still have mountain moving optimism?

Has your dream drifted beyond your reach? It doesn't always happen at once; it happens slowly.

Are you still pursuing something that is so lofty that is makes you afraid?

What happened to that version of you?

When we read the Word of God, we get to glean from mentors and heroes of faith that made mistakes we don't have to, acted imperfectly yet God still used them and provided examples of how to grow through what they went through. Peter models how to get our joy (strength) and fight back:

Grace and peace be multiplied to you in the knowledge of God and of Jesus our Lord, as His divine power has given to us all things that *pertain* to life and godliness, through the knowledge of Him who called us by glory and virtue, by which have been given to us exceedingly great and precious promises, that through these you may be partakers of the divine nature, having escaped the corruption *that is* in the world through lust. But also for this very reason, giving all diligence, add to your faith virtue, to virtue knowledge, to knowledge self-control, to self-control perseverance, to perseverance godliness, to godliness brotherly kindness, and to brotherly kindness love. For if these things are yours and abound, *you* will be neither barren nor unfruitful in the knowledge of our Lord Jesus Christ. For he who lacks these things is shortsighted, even to blindness, and has forgotten that he was cleansed from his old sins. Therefore, brethren, be even more diligent to make your call and election sure, for if you do these things you will never stumble; for so an entrance will be supplied to you abundantly into the everlasting kingdom of our Lord and Savior Jesus Christ (2 Peter 1:2-11 NKJV).

Grace and peace are multiplied to us as we recognize God. Grace is divine enablement, the ability and power that is beyond us, is activated in us when we recognize God. No matter what is happening, God is God. God has given us everything that pertains to life and godliness. It may feel like we don't have anything, but according to God's divine power, we have something. We're not left empty, and we don't have to allow our losses to have the final say. We sometimes think that God is only concerned about our spiritual life and not our natural life, but He has both dimensions worked out.

God won't put us in an environment without giving us the resources we need. He's trying to get us to know who we are because the moment we know who we are, we remember what we have. It's when we forget who we are that we forget what we possess, and we can't benefit from it. We're richer than we think. When we know what we have, we're no longer desperate and we're able to keep walking.

God called us through glory and to glory. We've been called to something incredible. There is power and resource already assigned to us. We are partakers of the divine nature which is a nature of growth and expansion. There are options, strategies, and breakthroughs in us because we are divine. We have an incredible opportunity. We can take the investment God has made in us and double down in life. We are here to lay hold of the opportunities that come with the breath in our body.

We determine the value of what we do. Being like God means being excellent and that is in our control. It takes work, diligence, and inspired action, but as we keep showing up, we move towards spiritual and life mastery. God wants us to pursue His brilliance; study, investigate, learn, and grow. Who did God save you to become? Isn't that worth exploring? We need to add something to our faith. Worship can be taking our life and representing God to the fullest because our destiny is greatness. This is what Peter talks about, tapping into the divine nature, and going from glory to glory in our daily lives.

Self-control is inner dominion, and you cannot be great without self-control. We must let the divine nature part of us dominate the other part of us. Self-control is learning how to master ourselves by our greater self. Greatness is not easy. Spiritual mastery and excellence are recognizing God and taking what He's given to us and being good stewards over it. When all we are is saved and don't go on to greatness, we give God back what He gave us rather than doing life with Him every day and becoming all He created us to be.

We will be tested but our lives can sow godliness amid darkness. Our growth and progress involve how well we can recognize God in any given moment. This is developed through intimacy, prayer and cultivating a relationship with God. The person that doesn't keep growing and building on the foundation God has given them, is short-sighted. When we don't lean into who God has called us to be we are pulled back into what He's delivered us from. We say no to hell by laying hold of heaven.

If we pursue what God guides us to pursue, we won't trip and fall. We will progress and progress is happiness. We never saw Jesus going backwards. That's the promise of God that's on our lives. If we lay our lives down for Him and commit to pursuing and being excellent, becoming the greatest version of who we are, we'll never cease to have favor. We are backed and secured by the kingdom that can't be shaken.

For much of my life, I didn't know that I could have a relationship with God. I didn't know what would happen if I read the Bible, in fact, I had every self-help book you can imagine on the shelf except the Bible. I found myself in a moment where I recognized that I had tried doing life to the best of my ability and hustled my way and I still felt like I was at a deficit and running on empty. I didn't want to limp through life anymore, waste time, get involved with the wrong people, stack achievements and keep starting over.

It took a while, but I was finally in a place where I could commit to at least exploring a relationship with God. I craved what Matthew writes about, the unforced rhythms of grace: "Are you tired? Worn out? Burned out on religion? Come to me. Get away with me and you'll recover your life. I'll show you how to take a real rest. Walk with me and work with me—watch how I do it. Learn the unforced rhythms of grace. I won't lay anything heavy or ill-fitting on you. Keep company with me and you'll learn to live freely and lightly" (Matthew 11:28-30 MSG).

What this looked like for me may sound basic to some and relatable to others. I decided that I wouldn't make excuses for why I didn't have a relationship with God, and do what I knew to do:

1. Go to a Christian store and buy a Bible and a devotional
2. Setup a daily devotion schedule and stick to it
3. Expect something will come from that time and remain consistent

I literally went to a Christian store and perused the aisles seeing if anything would jump out at me. I focused on what I needed and what questions I wanted answered. I wanted to know if I could hear God's voice for myself, how I was supposed to pray and what relationship even looked like, so I focused on devotionals that covered those themes. My schedule happened to be waking up early for two hours before work and spending time working through a section of a devotional, journaling takeaways, reading a Bible chapter each day, and reading a prayer to close out the quiet time. I didn't know what I was doing. I wasn't sure if anything would happen, if I was supposed to pray silently or out loud or if I would be transformed, but I was determined to keep showing up at least for a year. After a year, I'd planned to re-evaluate and at least would know I tried.

Shortly into my plan, I began noticing signs of growth. I noticed that as I was reading the Word, I was being drawn into what I was reading, and the Word was becoming alive and making sense to me. I noticed that I was writing and journaling like I'd never written before. I noticed that I started writing my own prayers and speaking them out loud. I noticed that I started to become emotional and cry when I hadn't cried in years. I noticed that what I'd always considered to be my intuition was Holy Spirit and God's Presence in my life. I noticed that I was starting to receive my next steps and that doors began opening quickly as I followed through.

One step was to get involved in church. I'd received an impression in my spirit to serve in a recovery ministry. I was led to attend a meet and greet event and introduce myself to the women's pastor over the recovery ministry. After meeting her, I was interviewed for a leadership position and a week later I was leading a recovery group. I like to say that God tricked me into my growth with a leadership position because He knew I could be trusted to show up for others and now I needed to also show up for myself and work the process. Throughout this Christ-centered recovery process, I learned how to put God first in my life and schedule everything else around Him. There was a lot that I had to let go of in that season, but it was also one of the most powerful growing seasons and blessed seasons of my life. I was allowing God to take the lead for the first time ever and I was becoming a transformed person in the process.

Transformation of the mind is taking back the crown. It teaches us to redirect our focus to the things that are within. It's knowing ourselves from our core. It's owning our destiny and expanding into our purpose. It's having the faith in ourselves to step into our future even if we have to go alone. We must keep believing that God really does want us healed and truly prosperous in every way. We also must keep pressing in for our healing and trust the Lord in the process.

Our growth process will demand we conquer ignorance, insecurity and then the lethargy and lack of initiative. We'll need to find the strength to step into our future. We'll be presented with opportunities to rethink the value of relationships and get to reintroduce ourselves to the world. We'll move from the superficial and dive deep to the core of who we are where our true value lies. We'll get to discover we're treasure in earthen vessels and the that the crown was never outside of us; the crown is at our core.

Who we're busy being, is who we're becoming. When we stop running, glorifying busy and choosing distractions, we have more space to work on our insides. When we work on our mind, will, emotions, heart attitudes, thoughts, beliefs, motives and intentions, the outside changes follow. Often, we're running after things that we want to win and receive awards for that actually don't exist:

- Never putting ourselves first
- Being the Busiest and the Most Stressed

- Being More worried and anyone because we care
- Being the one that slept the least
- Being the one that stayed on that weird diet for the longest
- Sacrificing our entire lives for others
- Being liked by everyone

All of these can seem harmless and tempting, but when we get still, become more aware and evaluate who we're being and becoming, it's eye opening. A list like this also indicates how easy it is to follow what we think we should do based on the culture we're exposed to without even examining why we do it in the first place. It requires courage and discipline to be still and go against what we think we should do. To say we're not disciplined or that it's too hard to change is not true. We have the fruit of self-control. We may not be using it, but you have it. What's in our power to do is in our power not to do. If we can say yes to something, we can say no to it. The choice is ours. The more we discipline ourselves, the more we can control ourselves. "For God did not give us a spirit of timidity *or* cowardice *or* fear, but [He has given us a spirit] of power and of love and of sound judgment *and* personal discipline [abilities that result in a calm, well-balanced mind and self-control]" (2 Timothy 1:7 AMP).

Sooner or later, we have to harness our power and focus it into one thing. Waiting on God is not about being lonely, it's about being prepared, it's our power position. The first victory we win is over ourselves. We can't do anything great just because we have natural talent, we want to until we first can manage ourselves, we won't be able to manage anything or anyone else. We're all preachers and we say a lot more with our actions than we do with our words.

Our lives are supposed to be salty. We're supposed to make other people thirsty to have a life like ours. If we really want to have victory in our lives, we're going to need to learn how to use discipline and self-control on a daily basis. Having it is not the same as using it. We need to toughen up. Getting our lives together requires a level of honesty you can't even imagine. There's nothing easy about realizing you're the one that's been holding yourself back the whole time. When we grow, we build the tenacity we need to be great in the world. If you really want to be a mature, strong and vibrant believer, you will have to through some things that are not very comfortable and learn to go through it, hold your head up high and not whine about it all the time. So often we try to get out of hard things by saying it's just too hard. That is just an excuse and it's a lie. If we want it bad enough, we will find a way. You can say no to anything if you know what the consequences will be if you don't. A lot of our problems are more our own fault than we like to think that they are. Until we take responsibility, nothing can be done about it. Now it's your turn.

Activation: We can't do anything apart from God. The key is to always ask God for help. The Word of God has power inherent in it. It's like taking medicine but it's medicine for your soul and there're unlimited free refills from God. You can't change by just trying. You admit your sin, repent, tell God you want to change and study in that area and be diligent.

Study the Bible in the area where you need to activate the fruit of self-control. If you have a problem with anger, studying success is not what you need. Look up verses about anger and meditate on them. Jot down your takeaways and pray for strength to release what is ill-fitting for you. God will never lead us to do anything that we cannot do. God will help you, you can do it, but probably not without discomfort.

This week: We're tempted to get into works as we start working the Word. Remember our relationship with God is what we're after—doing life with Him, not for Him! He is a place of trust. He is a place of love. He is a place of security, a place of safety. He is our answer.

"And you did not receive the "spirit of religious duty," leading you back into the fear of never being good enough. But you have received the "Spirit of full acceptance," enfolding you into the family of God. And you will never feel orphaned, for as He rises up within us, our spirits join Him in saying the words of tender affection, "Beloved Father" (Romans 8:15 TPT)!

Notice when you're tempted to work for approval or acceptance this week and choose again. Choose to look for God and you'll find Him, and with Him, everything else.

BECOME A STEADY FORCE

Therefore, my dear brothers, be steadfast, unmovable, always
excelling in the work of the Lord, because you know that
the work that you do for the Lord isn't wasted.

—1 Corinthians 15:58 ISV

There is a call for you, and it is from God. He has a plan for you, a destiny for you to fulfill. The Bible clearly teaches that the call of God is for the entire Body of Christ. Every gifting or anointing we have, comes from God, however, the enemy endeavors to distort the gift and turn it into his purpose, and in some cases, he is able to do that. God calls us by name and fills us with His Spirit in order that we might work as we're designed to. God fills His church with the Spirit for the power of workmanship. "For we are his workmanship, created in Christ Jesus for good works, which God prepared beforehand, that we should walk in them" (Ephesians 2:10 ESV). He has a special anointing that will make our minds as clear as can be, so we can receive the creative thoughts that He alone can give us. The call of God is powerful, life changing and very real.

Often before God calls us, faith is required. When Abraham was called, he obeyed by faith (see Hebrews 11:8). For some that is what God is doing right now, He's stirring up faith to help you obey. When we listen closely to the voice of God, we will be able to discern His call for our lives. It may not be in the most natural or easy arenas. He may even call you to lead people who don't want to be led, and you may need to learn lessons of patience. There are other times when He may call you to serve another and to assist in the fulfillment of someone else's dream.

God is interested in and looking for the person that He knows we can be. He can work in our lives in spite of our current doubts. When He calls us, it is not because of what we have done, but because of what He can do in and through us. He is looking for people who neither rely on, nor blame their past, but will willingly respond to the call of God. Some don't. The plan of God is for a revival of such major proportions that all will hear the good news of Jesus, and He will pour out His Spirit on all flesh. In order to bring in that kind of harvest, we need kingdom workers in all sectors of society. His Word is clear; He is calling. He called Abraham, Moses, Aaron, Gideon, Amos and the rich young ruler. Now He is calling us.

We can learn a lot about the call of God through studying how Saul and how David responded to it. In your quiet time, make a note to study their rulership in the Book of Samuel. Saul was a man of God, selected by God for his time. He demonstrated God's strength in his life. He did some awesome things; however, it wasn't very long in Saul's life before he lost his anointing as king and became disobedient. From Saul's story we can see that God is concerned about very specific obedience. He can give a word to us and even though we do most of it, if we don't do all of it, we may lose the Lord's blessing. Read and comprehend the Word of the Lord to Saul and to us, through Samuel:

> Has the Lord as great delight in burnt offerings and sacrifices, as in obeying the voice of the Lord? Behold, to obey is better than sacrifice, and to listen than the fat of rams. For rebellion is as the sin of divination, and presumption is as iniquity and idolatry. Because you have rejected the word of the Lord, he has also rejected you from being king (1 Samuel 15:22-23).

It's important to simply obey God, to take Him at His Word and allow the Holy Spirit to prepare us for the role God has for us. Hearing God and obeying God are ways we grow as children and obedience is vital if we want transformed lives. Complete surrender to the will of God is scary until we realize that with complete surrender comes complete peace in the most difficult circumstances. Jesus commissioned us to do what He did (participate in the miraculous) and even more (see John 14:12-14). We carry the power of God's kingdom as faith through love. We need to be willing to step out of the natural and start living in the supernatural of God. We need to be so heavenly minded that we are actually of some earthly good.

When we pay attention in our quiet time and encounters with God, we may also notice that God has a pattern. Moses spent time with God, received a vision and wrote down the ten commandments. Keeping a track record with God isn't about us, it's about legacy; it's about God doing something beyond us. God looks to and fro for someone to actually believe Him. "For the eyes of the Lord move to and fro throughout the earth so that He may support those whose heart is completely His" (2 Chronicles 16:9 AMP). Will He find you?

The pattern of tracking with God happens like this:

Praying→Hearing→Listening→Receiving→Believing

This is what it means to prepare the way for the Lord; to make space for God to give us what we need so we can track with Him and that often, is vision. Where there is no vision [no redemptive revelation of God], the people perish; but he who keeps the law [of God, which includes that of man]—blessed (happy, fortunate, and enviable) is he" (Proverbs 29:18 AMPC).

Any area that is hopeless in our lives is a result of no vision. No vision means, no prophetic word from God. The prophetic is God's way of communicating with us. It is a supernatural enabling by the Spirit of God to hear His voice and discern and interpret what that voice is saying. There are many ways to receive and relate with or experience God personally such as seeing (by the eyes of faith), hearing (could be an audible voice or still small voice), sensing, knowing (sometimes intuition or gut instinct), dreaming, or perceiving. God won't always communicate the same way in every season, so the main key is to stay in His faith and remain in constant contact with Him for His active wisdom and direction. What is the one thing that you know that God told you to do? Until it becomes the most valuable thing, you'll continue to wander and let what happens, happen.

Many don't really care about vision. They just go with whatever comes or they just seize the next opportunity as it comes. That isn't how God operates. He will give us a vision from the future and ask us to hold fast to it and remain obedient to each step in the process, stand and be steadfast, and persist even when everything else in our realities doesn't look like what He showed us and it seems as if it's not going to come to pass. God gives vision and it's valuable, but something can be valuable and not be your value. Read that again.

Vision needs to become our value. Declare: I will have vision for my future and all of my affairs. God is the Source of vision. This comes against what a lot of people will tell us, but our vision has to come from God. If a vision doesn't come from God, it is void. Vision is always vertical; you can never get a vision horizontally.

Everything that has ever been created was created from God to give Him glory. God has no lack of vision; He has lack of vessels. It's already created in heaven and He's waiting for a place to deposit it on earth so that it can come to pass. "For by Him all things were created in heaven and on earth, [things] visible and invisible, whether thrones or dominions or rulers or authorities; all things were created *and* exist through Him [that is, by His activity] and for Him" (Corinthians 1:16 AMP). You don't have to go searching around to every motivational speaker to catch a vision, all you have to do is get into God's Presence.

Vision is God's investment. When God gives someone on earth a vision, it's God's investment from heaven. He is trusting us with it. He doesn't invest not to see a return on investment. He invests for us to work it and multiply it. *Are you a good investment? Can God give you a glimpse of what He wants to do in the earth and you would be willing to pray it through, sow into it, give up other things for it, be steadfast around it, believe when no one else is believing? Are you a good investment? If God wants to get vision to the earth, can He do it through you? How will the kingdom of God advance if God can't drop His vision on us? How does He want you to represent Him to the world? Are you available to let God give you vision?* God doesn't do anything in the earth that He doesn't use a person to do, and vision is God's heavenly investment for an earthly return. What we've seen a lot is that God keeps dropping heavenly investments and He can't find people who would watch over them to see them actually happen in the earth. This needn't be our testimony.

Vision requires faith and obedience because it is always a risk and typically, the things that we are called to do are surrounded by resistance. There will be rejection, pessimists, haters, fear, guilt, doubt, self-sabotage, and intimidation. When we know that, we can beat it. This is what I've heard different mentors share, *"play the long game"* or in essence, run your own race with diligence no matter what because you're running your race from victory.

This revelation would have drastically changed my course if I'd know this before trying to find my way in the world. I can remember having a conversation with my father at a young age where he at one point said that he viewed me as an investment. I can't quite remember the context of the conversation, but the interesting thing is that I walked away with a perception that I wasn't a good investment. The way I received the message was that because he viewed me as in investment, it must mean that I'm not a good one yet. This is important to notice because we always receive and interpret things based on the level of our consciousness. That could have been an encouraging and inspiring message, but because of my level of consciousness at the time, I used it as a reason to perform and achieve in the world.

Strangely enough, I didn't know who I was or what I wanted to become for some time, I just knew what I didn't want to be anything like. My adoptive mother fell under the influence of alcoholism and lived with a lot of pain and suffering. As I studied her as a child, it stirred up a hunger in me to find the hope, power, and freedom I didn't see in my home. I innately knew that I could be pitiful or powerful, but I couldn't be both and yet, I didn't see role models teaching me how to be powerful. All I knew prior to my salvation experience was that there were certain things in my family that were going to stop with me, I was going to figure out how to break free of them and overcome them. You may know the story, but apart from God, I couldn't change things in my own strength and understanding. I needed a relationship with God and supernatural empowerment to tap into my healing and deliverance, a breaker anointing and my authentic voice.

My vision was deeply rooted, but it needed to be deeply rooted and grounded and God. I knew it was bigger than me, so it had to be God and also that it had God's heart for redemption and restoration all over it. I decided that I would stay connected to Him and allow Him to guide me in how to walk it out by faith one day at a time and one step at a time so that He could get all the glory as He radically changed my story.

Many times, because God can't find faith, He has to go to someone else who can catch His wind and run with it. We have to stop cowering in the face of what we see. We aren't supposed to go by sight, but by vision. Vision is what we see with our eyes closed. Do you see what He can do in your life? "So be careful how you listen; for whoever has [a teachable heart], to him *more* [understanding] will be given; and whoever does not have [a longing for truth], even what he thinks he has will be taken away from him" (Luke 8:18 AMP).

God wants to invest in you. Every vision needs a vehicle. Will you be the place He can sit to make that thing happen? Bring value to vision today so that you can choose differently. When you get a vision then Habakkuk 2:2 where we write the vision and make it plain comes into play. When we write a vision down, it becomes something that God can back on the earth. When we allow the spirit of God to give us a vision, help us do the things and stay consistent, then we can see things come to pass. If we listen, He'll give us vision in the valley and bring us from low to high.

Vision always makes us vulnerable, and vision must be visual, and it must be vocal. We need to open our mouth and declare it is so. If God said it, we believe it and if we believe it, we'll say it. We don't lose anything pointing to Him. If it did not happen how, we thought it would happen, it's for our good.

Vision is God's view. When it comes to vision God is asking us to come up higher and learn the character we'll need to lead at the next level. He gives us His view and then He asks us to live like the vision is vivid. This is where the enemy tries to make us believe it will never happen, that's why it needs to be plain. Down here we're living out what is in heaven. God has an intended future for us, but we need His view (see Jeremiah 29:11).

Vision has versions. We know and prophecy in part. God has a plan for our future, but we need to keep coming back to Him for His view. There is always more inside of us than what we have discovered. Where do you need God's view? Belief in the vision produces the results that take us beyond what we can see with our physical eyes. Think of the areas in your life that you've been drifting, and you need to get rooted. God wants you to become a steady force—something that can stand and withhold no matter what storm comes. He wants us to always be rooted and grounded in Him.

When you bring value to vision, it changes the way you treat it. Mark down the words that God says. We may have no idea how they will happen, when they will happen or even why they will happen, but God sometimes gives us glimpses that He wants us to jot down. Put it on God so that He can get the glory.

Activation: Below is a Jesus Wheel from the *God's Vibes Matter: Co-Laboring with God* book that takes you on a deeper dive into journeying with God, specifically in each of the eight segments. The key is to jumpstart your visioning process with God. Where have you been drifting? Where do you want God to stabilize you? Look at each segment and put a number (from 1-10, 10 being totally yielded to God and full of faith and 1 being I haven't even invited God into this yet) in each based on you what you sense. Which area are you called to invest in now? Take that before God in your quiet time and allow Him to reveal a vision for what that area looks like with Him. The great thing is, as one area changes, all of them inevitably do. This is a great tool to work with a coach. For more information on coaching visit www.julianapage.com

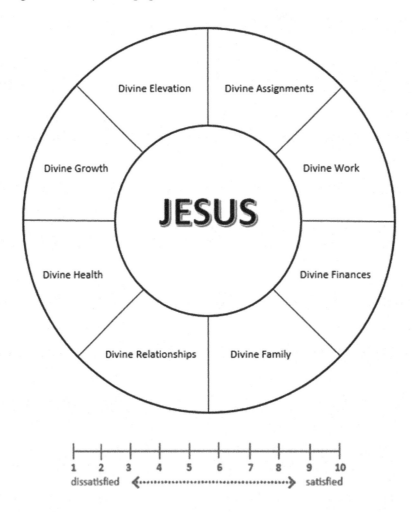

Free Flow: What are the things that God has shown you? What are the visions that He's given you for your family, for your marriage, for your busines that you marked down? What are the things that you received that you believed enough to write down?

This Week: Reflect back on the name God has given you. Based on this name, ask God: If I could fulfil all you've purposed and planned for me and I could trust You would provide all the resources, connections, and support, what would that look like?

Complete the following with Holy Spirit—Dream BIG with God!

I am becoming…

I am creating…

I am contributing…

I am possessing…

I am traveling to…

I am being…

PLAY THE LONG-GAME

I am not saying this because I am in need, for I have learned to be content
whatever the circumstances. I know what it is to be in need, and I know
what it is to have plenty. I have learned the secret of being content in any
and every situation, whether well fed or hungry, whether living in plenty
or in want. I can do all this through him who gives me strength.

—Philippians 4:11-13 NIV

*S*ome believers experience the power of God more than others. Some see God's
supernatural activity so clearly in their lives because they've decided that the only appropriate
response to Him is complete obedience. They are committed to obeying His leading no
matter how absurd His instructions may be or how long the process is. This kind of response
lays the groundwork for God to do incredible things in their lives and greatly supports them
in ruling and reigning.

How we choose to respond to God is more important than hearing from Him. Abraham
was called *"the friend of God"* not because He heard God's voice but because he was committed
to obeying God's voice. Time and time again, God demonstrated His ability in and through
Abraham because Abraham was willing to obey whatever God told him. The worst thing we can
do and the quickest way to become insensitive is to ignore a prompting or an impression from
the Holy Spirit. We must commit ourselves to listening to God for the purpose of responding to
what He says and not allow ourselves to hear without responding.

This may require keeping the end in mind and planning to obey God in advance. We often
want to see God's supernatural activity, but how many times have we forfeited God's blessing in
our lives? We usually refuse to follow God's direction when we think what we must give up is
greater than what we will gain. As a result, we miss God's blessing, experience His judgement,
and break the intimacy that allows our spiritual ears to hear what He has to say to us in the
future. In the short run, it may appear that our way is best, but we will soon see that obedience
would have given access to His supernatural power. Obedience will always produce benefits that
far outweigh the consequences of disobedience. When we choose to obey, we find God rewards
us with His power, Presence, and supernatural blessing.

As we seek to discern God's voice and respond appropriately, we can become frustrated
because it seems God is steering us away from our cherished goals. We don't always know or

consider what major adjustments this surrender might entail. If we don't prepare to modify our plans, we will end up more frustrated and overwhelmed. Deciding to adjust our lives in obedience to God requires surrender. Proverbs 19:21 reveals that only God's purposes will prevail. Any plan we devise on our own will not reap eternal dividends. If we want to see God operating in our lives, we must adopt His plans and accept His invitation to be part of them.

It's not that we will never see our dreams become reality, it's more that the Holy Spirit is at work in us to change our desires to match up with God's desires. We must keep our plans flexible and never make concrete plans without leaving room for God to do something different. It's comforting to have a plan B waiting when obedience isn't convenient anymore, but God desires that we "burn our ships," annihilate any other means of departure, and throw ourselves wholeheartedly into what He asks of us. Scripture has a name for believers who desire to hear from God but have a plan B waiting in the wings: double-minded (see James 1:7-8). James says if we are double minded, we should expect to receive nothing from the Lord.

When we are not hearing from the Lord, we can ask if doublemindedness is the cause. Complete obedience to God requires a commitment to modify and change our plans at a moment's notice. This requires radical faith and radical trust in God. It can also seem frightening unless we know God is good and kind. He has our best interest in mind and has a plan for is that is for our good (see Jeremiah 29:11). When we give ourselves wholly to Him, we can be sure He will give us strength to accomplish His mission.

The abundant life God has promised us is expansive (see John 10:10). It is in our best interest to play the long game as we walk out and steward what God has entrusted to us. If we want to really play the long game, then we need to know what the short game looks like. Often it looks like telling ourselves why we deserve to not show up and procrastinating, making excuses, taking shortcuts, leaning on our own power, and understanding, and doing what feels best in the moment versus what we know is best and being consistent. There are a lot of reasons why we chose to play the short game and why we settle. Anyone that wants our best and has our best interest at heart wouldn't encourage this. God hasn't called us to play the short game. He's called us to rule and reign in life. He's called us to play the long game and live a life of faith. He wants to equip us to go the distance, in fact He created us to go the distance.

In my life, I've been reminded far more times than I'd like, to play the long game when it comes to visions of the divine work, businesses and ministries God has shown me. Like our character development, our work development has many learning curves, peaks, and valleys that we don't always anticipate. In my case, there were many things that I didn't realize I was unprepared for. For example, when I decided to complete my training to be a professional life coach, I was twenty-three. Because I felt so strongly that this is what I was being led to commit to while in graduate school, I didn't see that as an issue. It was when I finished all my training and my graduate degree and went out to take massive action in the world that I learned that ongoing learning was the path.

There is a belief in the world that once we finish school for example, there will be companies and clients waiting to work with us. Unfortunately, this is just not so. The reality is, we invest lots of money, time, energy, and resources into our development and still are not prepared for our future. Often, we won't feel qualified for what God calls us to do so it is important to recognize that God qualifies the called (see 1 Corinthians 1:27-29). Once I awakened to the reality that ongoing investing was par for the course, I became smarter about it. There are a plethora of tools, trainings, programs, and courses available in the world, but not all of them will deliver a return on investment and it's crucial to pray and obey particularly with the resources God has given us to steward. While for some time I was frustrating that I felt like I was ready for what God had shown me, and resisted going to the trainings, mentors, and programs, I came to a space where I changed my mindset and attitude. First, if I was ready, I'd be in God's timing walking out the fullness of what I'd seen. If I wasn't, there was still more for me to learn and I was to be faithful where I was. Secondly, it was God who led me to the mentors and development I needed, and He was also the one providing for it, therefore, what really did I have to complain about? The long game often looks like this:

Learning → Training → Assignment

Until we are ready for the assignment, we're either learning or in training. If we think we're ready but haven't received confirmation from the Lord, we're still in training. It helps to see this because then we can show up fully where God has us. Now, as a coach, I invest in whatever I need because I know with God, I'm a good investment and I will be able to apply the wisdom and development He leads me to with greater power and authority. There isn't a one size fits all formula, program or training that fully prepares us for what's next. I believe when we're ready God connects us with the teaches, programs, mentors, and knowledge that we need to grow in His wisdom, stature and favor with God and man (see Luke 2:52). I invest in coaches, therapists and other experts that can help me because I know that I have blind spots and I'm also committed to walking my talk. Unless God gives me peace about moving forward with additional development or work, I don't move until I have peace and if I don't feel peace, I acknowledge that it's either a no or a not right now and I keep moving forward. I've found that it's also key to keep God first because all wisdom and knowledge flow from Him and He often uses people to support us but not always. Sometimes He wants us to lean on and rely on Him alone; that's where faith comes in.

The Book of Hebrews (see Hebrews 11) teaches us what faith in action looks like and gives us the key to playing the long game. It's one word, faith. Faith is confidence in what we hope for, the assurance about what we do not see. Faith is about future and faith is about the unseen. When it comes to our prayer life for example, there is no recipe for perfect prayers. We can however inject our prayers with faith for the future and look beyond the present and start to speak faith over what we do not see. Faith isn't designed to just be an idea but part of the DNA of who we are.

Hebrews 11 is a list of heroes whose lives are central to the saving power of Jesus. Their stories are connected to our story. "All these people were still living by faith when they died" (Hebrews 11:13 NIV). This scripture redefines what the long game is. These heroes of the faith died while they were still believing for what God showed them. What is the long game for you? Could it actually be longer than this life? Here on earth isn't always where we receive it, but where we choose to believe it. We get to decide whether or not we will spend our lives believing the promises of God and holding onto His truth knowing that this life is not the totality of the promise.

When we misinterpret the long game, we're disappointed when our expectations are unmet. What would happen if we redefined the long game in our lives? When we entrust our lives to God, He empowers us to play the long game. To play the long game we must be Holy Spirit empowered. This is being aware of where our strength comes from. It's acknowledging and giving credit to where credit is due. When we surrender our life to Christ, something inside of us shifts and it changes everything. Our eyes don't have to be inwardly focused, and we don't have to worry about what others think of us. We're more concerned about what others know about Him and others' eyes being opened to the Source of strength that is the power of the Holy Spirit.

There is a coming day when Christ will return for His church and He will redeem all of humanity, but until that moment, the Holy Spirit seals us. "And you also were included in Christ when you heard the message of truth, the gospel of your salvation. When you believed, you were marked in him with a seal, the promised Holy Spirit, who is a deposit guaranteeing our inheritance until the redemption of those who are God's possession—to the praise of his glory" (Ephesians 1:13-14).

God has written His name on us. Don't touch him. Don't touch her. No weapon formed against us shall prosper. We are covered by the blood of Jesus and sealed by His name. He has sealed us until He comes back for us. The Holy Spirit is a guarantee of our inheritance. Our inheritance is what we're waiting for, not what we hold right now. God the Father, through Jesus has given us the Holy Spirit here on earth as a guarantee of our inheritance to come. The Holy Spirit counsels us, comforts us and He reminds us of all the things that Jesus said. The Holy

Spirit produces the fruit of the spirit. The Holy Spirit bears fruit inside of us, actually stretches us, shapes our character, our desires, our intentions, our motivations specifically so that we can endure and so that we can play the long game, also known as long suffering. Long suffering also known and forbearance, is seeking God first so that He can direct our path. This is way better than making our own plans.

To play the long game we must be faith inspired. Faith is seeing something that other people just don't see. Creatives know the inspiration process is all about seeing something that causes them to want to create something that no one have ever seen before. Faith inspires. We're inspired by more than just right now and what the world would tell us we need to achieve happiness, peace, and success. We also know that there's always a temptation to play the short game.

We see this through the story of Jacob and Essau. Essau gives Jacob the birth right for stew. He sacrifices his long-term inheritance for his short-term appetite. How often do we choose our flesh instead of our faith? How often do we take the easy street, the street everyone else says we should go, but deep in our heart we have a conviction of what we do not see, but we silence the conviction because it's faster results. That's not the way of faith. We live our lives as seeds to be sown for generations to come. Through the eyes of Christ, we can see by faith the future and the unseen and if we can see it then we will sow it.

When we're able to look beyond the here and now and we're able to look through the lens of heaven, and see an inheritance waiting on the other side for us, it becomes a no brainer to invest our lives in the kingdom. What will you have invested your life into? His Word is our inspiration. There's no limit to what He will do in and through us if we can't decide that we see it.

The long game must be generationally focused. "These were all commended for their faith, yet none of them received what had been promised, since God had planned something better for us so that only together with us would they be made perfect" (Hebrews 11:39-40 NIV). God is telling a multi-generational story. This is History. Can you see it? We can sow our lives, serve, and grow when we get our eyes off ourselves and on what God is actually doing. This means being intentional about what we're actually sowing and who will reap the seeds. Our lives then become an offering. "If they had been thinking of the country they had left, they would have had opportunity to return. Instead, they were longing for a better country—a heavenly one. Therefore God is not ashamed to be called their God, for he has prepared a city for them" (Hebrews 11:15-16).

Generational focus does not desire to go back to where we've already been. There will always be an opportunity for us to go back to our comfort zone. Our longing will lead, direct, and sustain us as we move forward. Can you see beyond your own lifespan? What will our legacy be? Will His power embolden you and fortify every season of your life?

Can you see eternity? Our spirit was created to play the long game. What do you see in the future? Is it a faithful God? We're surrounded by a great crowd of witnesses. There are times where we must be intentional about seeking God out. Focus. Can you see your life being used as a seed? "I pray that the eyes of your heart may be enlightened in order that you may know the hope to which he has called you, the riches of his glorious inheritance in his holy people" (Ephesians 1:18). This life is all about what we believe.

Activation: During the long game, at times it's challenging to discern how to approach a particular area or season. Use the chart below to evaluate where you are on the area or areas of your life that you sense are being highlighted.

Phase 1: Play the Hand

This is a time to be fully in the moment. It is mostly harmonious, optimistic, and determined. While this stage is mostly associated with success, it can also bring up question around what to do next. This is a time to remain solution-focused and clear.

Phase 2: Toss In

This is an ending. It can seem like an isolation or hibernation time with lower levels of energy and taking action. It's important to think outside of the box and lean into growth. How have you grown from this?

Phase 3: Shuffle

This is a time-out phase to emotionally heal, reflect and research and find new direction that will lead to a renewal and re-energizing. This is a time to turn inwards with God and evaluate core values and priorities. What do you have fresh hope to begin?

Phase 4: Deal

This is an action time. It's a time for experimenting, training, and networking, all of which are an implementation of what's developed in the shuffle phase. This is a time of confidence and stretching to new heights. What do you need to follow through on?

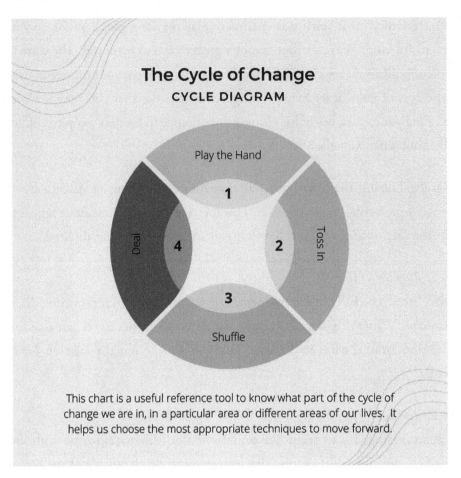

The Cycle of Change

CYCLE DIAGRAM

This chart is a useful reference tool to know what part of the cycle of change we are in, in a particular area or different areas of our lives. It helps us choose the most appropriate techniques to move forward.

Journal out your thoughts and inspired actions.

This week: Look up the following verses. What do they say about obeying God?

Exodus 15:26-27

Exodus 23:22

Deuteronomy 31:12

Luke 8:18

John 14:15

What is God asking you to do?

Write a prayer responding to God's commands to you:

Part Two

DEVELOP SELF-MASTERY

I have the right to do anything," you say—but not everything is beneficial. "I have the right to do anything"—but I will not be mastered by anything.

—1 Corinthians 6:12 NIV

*W*hy is it that so many people seem to start so well and then their journey seems to end abruptly? Not the end of their lives, but the end of their dreams, their success and their influence and credibility because their life just fell apart. One of the greatest challenges when you're a follower of Jesus is trying to understand what it means to be a disciple. The reality is, the things we're often told to do which are important, to spend time in prayer, to spend time in the Scriptures, to spend time in the church, they're critical but they're not the essential ingredients that allow a person to sustain their journey for the long haul.

There are essential practices in the lives of men and women that thrive and that develop resilience and the capacity not only to start well but to finish well. The concept that these men and women embrace is called self-mastery. Self-mastery seems like it sounds as if it violates the core of faith, when Christ is supposed to have mastery over our lives, but self-mastery comprises disciplines and structures that allow us to optimize our God-given potential and calling. It's also vital to our spiritual journeys.

Through self-mastery we can redirect what would seem to be dysfunctional. With focus, intention and discipline for example, ADHD channeled creatively can become an art form. Behind every expression of greatness and genius is discipline, self-control, and self-mastery. Why would we think that our Spirit, the core essence of our being would require anything less than the highest level of self-mastery?

Self-mastery is about living out the abundant life Jesus spoke of in John 10:10. It means that we are alive on purpose, for a purpose and our purpose is to live like it. We are at the cause instead of the effect of our lives. We take our influence seriously and decide to be powerful because inherently we know, we can be pitiful or powerful, but we can't be both. We learn to align with God and resonate at His frequency in the world. We decide to live lives where we control ourselves and show up without having to control anything or anyone. We hold the keys to balancing the light and the darkness in the world. It can be scary at times, but we must choose to shine. As powerful people we take responsibility for our lives and choices; our job is to control ourselves. As a result, we consciously and deliberately create the environments in which we went to live. We set the standard and consistently act in loving, respectful, and honorable ways. Life doesn't just happen, we create it.

I remember really being intrigued by this concept of living as a creator and creating reality when I read the language on my graduate school pamphlet. It said something like, "make your dreams a reality." I thought, I have no idea how to do that or what that looks like, but surely these people speak my language and can help me. While I learned a ton, this was before I discovered self-mastery. It was a few years after graduate school, after peeling back more layers on my development journey that I faced a hard truth, unhealed parts of myself were holding me back from living out the fullness of my potential. I could gain more and more knowledge, but until I started working on my inner man, a broken inside would still create a broken outside.

It was after my salvation that I was empowered to tap into my new nature and was given the courage to go deeper into my healing. From a Christ-centered recovery program to inner healing certifications and many things in between, I began to discover the power of repentance, renewing my mind, speaking my world, activating faith, and surrounding myself with spirit-filled community and accountability. This journey continues today but it is now one that I am passionate about because I know the deep wells of strength and compassion I continue to break into and draw from. Now these practices are integrated not only in my self-mastery practices but in my coaching, training, and ministering as well.

The freer we become, the more we can release this to others. While each of us can do many things well, there is only one thing that we can truly master, and that is being ourselves. We are divine masterpieces, and when we tap into our true nature, our light is revealed to the world. The Bible says that when we are born again, we become new creatures in Christ. The "new creature" the Apostle Paul is referring to is the inwards man. "Therefore we do not lose heart. Though outwardly we are wasting away, yet inwardly we are being renewed day by day" (2 Corinthians 4:16 NIV). In other words, old things are passed away in the inward man and all things have become new. That means the sin nature in our spirits has been done away with. The man on the inside has become a new man in Christ and has a new nature—the nature of God.

It's important to be aware that we don't just arrive, we will always have the flesh to deal with and we will have to keep it under the dominion of our spirit—the man on the inside. Paul said, "But I discipline my body and bring *it* into subjection, lest, when I have preached to others, I myself should become disqualified" (1 Corinthians 9:27 NKJV). We must crucify our flesh; that means we must keep the flesh under. God is not going to do it for us.

As part of our self-mastery journey, we can also learn to appropriate all the spiritual blessings we've already been blessed with. We can learn to receive the fullness of our inheritance in Christ in this life. Part of our redemption in Christ for example, includes that fact that we have become the righteousness of God in Christ. We are not righteous in ourselves; but Christ has become our righteousness and as long as we are in Christ, God sees us as righteous. We need to be conscious of what we expose ourselves to and what we allow to have power over us. If anything has power over us, it has authority over us, it rules and dominates us. We're not to live under the devil's authority or anything that has to do with his kingdom. We have been delivered from his authority, but we need to act like it. We're instructed to not even give the devil place in our lives (see Ephesians 4:27). That means, the devil can't take any place unless we let him. It's being doers of God's Word that empowers us to prosper in life.

To get to our core, we must heal emotionally from the trauma of our history and experiences. We have to think about what we're thinking and purge the poison of the propaganda that has only served to limit us. The good news is, the more we pour God's truth in, the lies will rise to the top, spill over and go down the drain. We have to get uncomfortable and begin to manifest our true greatness.

Maybe for you, it's not that you haven't practiced some of the things that you've learned strengthen your spiritual journey, but perhaps you've lacked some basic structures in your life and discipline that would allow you to have self-mastery so that you can make the breakthroughs you need to live the life God created you to live.

If no one told you, know this, we were created to write the story of our lives. God will teach us how to write it in a way where the story is written with the imagination of God. There is no level of spirituality where we will ever be allowed to abdicate responsibility for ourselves. There is no level of spirituality where giving God ownership of our lives allows us to no longer take ownership over our own lives.

Ownership is the beginning and end of our ability to create the life that we have longed for; the life that God created us to live. If we have an improper relationship with personal ownership, we will never be able to deal with whatever we faced in the past, the challenges we have in the present and the dreams we want to create in the future.

Lack of personal ownership comes with consequences. The consequences of Adam and Eve's choices that are now affecting the rest of humanity, but we've often been taught that after the fall we can no longer make good, wise choices. This is not the case. In Genesis we find God having a conversation with Cain and letting him know that the decision is in his hands. "So the Lord said to Cain, "Why are you angry? And why has your countenance fallen" (Genesis 4:6 NIV). Cain not only had the power to choose what is right but what is wrong. He had the power to choose what would destroy and what would create. This highlights that there is never a place in the Scriptures where the narrative of human choice is taken away from us.

God was teaching Cain to take mastery over his life. The idea of self-mastery is God's idea. While we make thousands on thousands of choices in our lives, not every choice in our life has the same weight. There are choices that have a greater impact and affect every choice we make going forward. That's the power of the choice of choosing Jesus. When we choose Him, that choice affects every choice in our lives going forward.

When we make destructive choices and choices that violate who God's created us to be, those choices have consequences and momentum. They have force and it affects our future. Mastery begins with ownership; with taking responsibility for our lives. For some this is a complex process because who you are right now is the outcome of not choice that you've made alone, but choices that other people have made. There are some that have been devastated by choice that others have made; choices that were made when you were young, innocent, fragile and vulnerable. The choices that other people have made that impacted your life may have such a detrimental destructive effect on you that you feel that your life is out of control and it can cause you to live your entire life with a sense of victimization that it's not right and it's not fair.

What we must embrace somewhere along the way is that even if it's not right or fair or our fault, it is our responsibility. It makes life unbalanced in the scale of what some have to deal with, and some have to carry such wounding, abuse, neglect and pain and some may not even understand the full extent of it but feel paralyzed. It doesn't help when someone acknowledges it's not our fault, but it is our responsibility. Sometimes what we need to hear is a hard truth. We must hear the hard truth that while someone else may have caused the damage in our lives, only we can choose to move past the pain.

When we invite Jesus into our lives, He becomes the one who can heal the wounds we can't. He repairs what is broken within us that we can't repair ourselves. It is God who becomes the one who can move us out of our past into our future, but don't let that confuse you. That doesn't remove from you, your responsibility because even then you have to choose to allow for God to do that. Even then, you have to ask God to do that in your life. Even then you have to go through the painful process of healing that God will send you through.

The more we take responsibility for our lives the more we'll find the power to create the life we long for. We can see the shift in ownership from the very beginning with Adam and Eve:

> When the woman saw that the fruit of the tree was good for food and pleasing to the eye, and also desirable for gaining wisdom, she took some and ate it. She also gave some to her husband, who was with her, and he ate it. Then the eyes of both of them were opened, and they realized they were naked; so they sewed fig leaves together and made coverings for themselves.

> Then the man and his wife heard the sound of the Lord God as he was walking in the garden in the cool of the day, and they hid from the Lord God among the trees of the garden. ⁹ But the Lord God called to the man, "Where are you?"

He answered, "I heard you in the garden, and I was afraid because I was naked; so I hid."

And he said, "Who told you that you were naked? Have you eaten from the tree that I commanded you not to eat from?"

The man said, "The woman you put here with me—she gave me some fruit from the tree, and I ate it."

Then the Lord God said to the woman, "What is this you have done?"

The woman said, "The serpent deceived me, and I ate" (Genesis 3:6-13).

God's love demands freedom. We simply cannot have love without free will. If man and woman didn't have the freedom to choose, they wouldn't have the freedom to love and to trust, to be truly and fully alive. The beginning of the story with Adam and Eve begins with God giving us the power to choose. He told us to take responsibility for this planet and to be the stewards of it; he gave us ownership.

In the Book of Genesis, we see the first consequential act of severing relationship with God, blame. Adam and Eve no longer took responsibility for their choices and displaced responsibility. Whether we embrace responsibility or displace it, reveals a lot about us. Out of the wrong choices and instead of taking responsibility and ownership for their lives, Adam and Eve began to blame one another. Do you blame anyone for your life?

How many times in our lives do we create a language for deflecting responsibility? Sometimes there are people to blame. We can look back on our lives and find people who deserve to be blamed, but as long as we blame someone else, not just for that act, moment or experience, but when we blame someone for our lives, we are abdicating the power to change our lives. The reality is, whoever is responsible has the power to bring the change. As long as we refuse to take ownership for our lives, we will never take hold of the power to change our lives. We need to take ownership of who we are and who we're becoming. Our response to life has more power to shape who we are than what life can throw at us.

As we take ownership over our lives, we find the power to change our lives. Our circumstances are never the reasons for our failures, it's our failure to choose well. God holds us responsible for the choices we're making in the midst of all the uncertainty. What choices are you making so that your circumstances aren't always shaking your outcomes? What choices are you making so that you can have a greater impact on your circumstances? The choices we make will create the future we will live in. There is no more spiritual act than to choose. Our actions are the arena of prayer not our outcomes.

If we're not willing to let God change how we choose, we can't ask God to change the consequences of those choices. The real evidence of spiritual maturity is that we stop involving God in the consequence and we start involving God in the choices. It's in the choices where we have to have self-mastery. Instead of choosing the choices that are easy or making the choice that gives us temporary satisfaction, we can make the choice where the momentum doesn't steal the future, but it actually creates it.

We need to take mastery over the influence we have on the world around us. Our lives are interconnected and our choices either hurt or help someone else. When we take mastery, of who we are and who we're becoming that's when we begin living at the highest level of self-mastery. How much ownership do you have over your life right now? Look at the different arenas in your life and begin to identify all of those areas of your life that are not an expression of who want to be. Ask yourself what choices you need to make to take ownership in that area of your life. Where have you allowed yourself to be a victim?

Instead of blaming someone else, take ownership and begin to step into the creation of a new life. As long as you don't forgive and hold onto bitterness, they still have power over you. Men and women who persevere and show resilience, who aren't just great starters but finishers and live a full life, have taken ownership over their lives. Give no one else the power over the creation of who you are but Jesus. Let Him do a work in you that you can't do for yourself and move toward self-mastery. We need God to really become the person we long to be and live the life we long to live.

Activation: The path to mastering anything, whether it's your habits, your job, your relationships, your family, or your finances, comes from committing to an active relationship with God. Ask Holy Spirit:

1. Who can I connect with that can be a mentor/model whose life speaks and bears much fruit around what I'm called to?

2. What would you have me immerse myself in to learn and gain relevant knowledge in this season?

3. What lifestyle habits do I need to have in place to repeat your principles and develop my character?

This week: God can use anyone, anytime, anywhere to be a spiritual leader. Spiritual leaders can exercise their gifts anywhere, not just in the church. Spiritual leaders understand that God is their leader, and they seek His will and adjust their lives to Him. True spiritual leaders revere God more than fear man and practice self-mastery.

Sometimes before we can embrace new habits we need to repent from bad habits and lies we've partnered with. Repentance means to change the way we think. Once we identify the lies, we believe and the influence those lies have on our lives we break agreements with them. We then ask Holy Spirit to come and tell us the truth. A model repentance prayer could look like:

In the name of Jesus, I renounce the lie that _____.
I nail it to the cross of Jesus Christ and send it away from me, never to return again. Holy Spirit, what truth would you like to give me in its place?

Write down what the Holy Spirit tells you and repeat this prayer for each individual lie that comes up.

Now, cultivate the habits of a spiritual leader. Use the list below to redefine your leadership.

Jesus is our model. He had the following habits:

- Cultivating and maintaining a close relationship with God
- Hearing from God and moving others to God's agenda
- Frequent and fervent prayer
- Acting based on His identity
- Setting a clear example for His followers
- Mentoring and investing in future leaders
- Loving every person
- Counting the cost of serving God and willingly submitting to God's will

Take it further: Don't let stubborn beliefs get the best of you. Turn any limiting beliefs you have into liberating affirmations. Speak forth your royal decrees and declarations for these habits. Look up scripture verses that align with each habit you've listed and decree and declare it shall be establish in your life by God's power and for His glory.

Manage Your Energy

For this I toil, struggling with all his energy that
he powerfully works within me.

—Colossians 1:29 ESV

We often hear of time management but far more important than time management is energy management. Often, we don't think of ourselves as energy creatures but we both expend energy, and we have to replenish that energy. The language of energy is becoming more wildly accepted and normalized in culture. It's one of those words we use to compliment someone, "you have such great energy." We can also pick up on the energy in different rooms or a vibe someone gives off. Years ago, the language of energy seemed esoteric but now we have energy bars and energy drinks, and we have an entire industry around it. That's also why it's important to recognize that only God's vibes matter.

The reality is that everything is energy, it's just energy moving at different speeds and expressing itself in different ways. What will change a moment and transform it into a moment that has momentum is the amount of energy you bring into that moment.

Jesus was someone with unlimited energy. We find that when He was fully man, He actually expended energy and even experienced the power that was in Him actually go out from Him to someone else.

Now when Jesus returned, a crowd welcomed him, for they were all expecting him. Then a man named Jairus, a synagogue leader, came and fell at Jesus' feet, pleading with him to come to his house because his only daughter, a girl of about twelve, was dying.

As Jesus was on his way, the crowds almost crushed him. And a woman was there who had been subject to bleeding for twelve years, but no one could heal her. She came up behind him and touched the edge of his cloak, and immediately her bleeding stopped.

"Who touched me?" Jesus asked.
When they all denied it, Peter said, "Master, the people are crowding and pressing against you."

But Jesus said, "Someone touched me; I know that power has gone out from me." Then the woman, seeing that she could not go unnoticed, came trembling and fell at his feet. In the presence of all the people, she told why she had touched him and how she had been instantly healed. Then he said to her, "Daughter, your faith has healed you. Go in peace (Luke 8:40-48 NIV).

There is a transference of energy from Jesus to this woman. Jesus interacted with so many people, but this interaction was captured as significant. It seemed that the transference of energy required intention. The woman pressed toward Jesus and touched Him with intention. She doesn't even get to His body; she just touches His garment. This moment is highlighted so we can see how energy transfers and how the power of God brought healing to the woman who reached out and asked for help.

We are both consumers and conduits of energy. We both expend energy every day, and we also consume energy every day. A lot of us look to external sources of energy to get us going throughout the day. We go to coffee, pre-workout, donuts, sugar, breakfast tacos, drinks, energy bars and even social media for a "fix." Life has different effects on us, and it changes the energy dynamics inside of us. We need to be careful if we're only doing things that drain or cost energy and we're not doing things that replenish energy. We all expend and replenish energy differently.

There are two arenas where we expend energy: in our inner world and the outer world. In those worlds there are epicenters that consume energy. These are problems, crisis, and challenges. Long before we ever have to face a problem, we expend energy trying to solve it. Have you noticed? Often our ratio is way off in the amount of time we spend worrying versus solving problems.

Our relationships are another area. These are some of the highest consumers of our energy. Navigating relationships is exhausting and yet, the people in our lives also bring the greatest amount of beauty, joy and fulfilment. Unhealthy relationships suck us dry of all the energy we have. Everything in life can be going great and if we have unhealthy relationships, we will feel as if we have no energy for life. We can move with deliberation to create healthy relationships in our lives. It's one of the reasons Jesus talks so much about forgiveness and the destructive power of bitterness. When there is health in our relationships, they become a source of energy.

Work is another energy consumer. It can seem entirely about what we're producing in our life. Often our jobs become a source that only consume our energy rather than replenish our energy. If work is stealing energy, it may be unfulfilling and not in alignment with God's purpose for our lives, it may not be challenging, or it doesn't give us a sense that we're doing something that matters in the world. When we find work that matches who we are and what we're created to do in life it energizes us. If that's not possible, we can bring meaning to our work or find meaning outside of our work. Sometimes we're just financing your dreams and your future.

The other place where energy is consumed is through negative emotions. These will eat up more of our energy than anything else in our lives. The Bible cannot be clearer that we should release things like bitterness, envy, greed and unforgiveness. These emotions will destroy us. Love, hope, and faith are energizing. Energy comes in motion. If we find ourselves lacking the passion and energy to live our lives to the fullest, the starting point is to get moving and serve someone else.

There have been many seasons where it felt like all I was doing was expending energy. I began to think that that must be how I was wired, but it was exhausting. Right after I'd finished my life coaching training and graduate school, I decided to drive across the country and start checking off things I was led and inspired to do rather than what I "should" or "had" to. As scary as that was, I was more afraid of what would happen if I didn't do this.

When I started settling in, in addition to launching a life coaching practice from scratch, I decided that I needed to make a list of things that energize me and fed my soul. One of the things I stumbled into was DJ school. I had no idea that this was a thing, but while on a whim grabbing a tea, I walked by a DJ school and made a note to make inquires. I found out that the class was six weeks, we'd learn how to DJ and one of the final projects would be DJing live at a venue for graduation.

How was this even a thing? Of course, I signed up. On the first day, I didn't realize I needed to have a DJ name and the owner called me *"Vibes."* What's neat about that was my coaching practice was called *Vibes Matter*, which he couldn't have known. It felt like a gentle affirmation and a reminder to pay attention to the energy I'm giving and receiving. The experience was an adventure and fun and I was glad I stepped way outside of my comfort zone. Later I learned that while, everything is energy and vibes matter in that what we think, affects how we feel and then how we act, when I came to know the Lord, I soon discovered that only His vibes matter. In other words, I wanted to know His thoughts, principles, promises, Words and build my life on His foundation. If I didn't, what really could I say was my solid foundation? How would I discern good things from God things? How would I exercise wisdom with energy?

We're not just supposed to expend energy, we're supposed to make sure that we are also receiving the power that we need. Jesus says we will receive His Spirit and He says we'll receive Dunamis which isn't our strength or ability but rather to His power through us. It is His power alone that keeps us, while forming our character as we glorify Him. When we live in communion with Him in the Presence of God, and we dwell with God and His Spirit energizes us, we receive the Dunamis to live the life that God has created us to live.

Often, we look for energy from every other source than the One that can really empower us. It's God's energy, His Presence, His Spirit that is the only Source that can powerfully refuel us. As we live our lives in alignment with His purpose for our lives, we find life energizing. We start to see problems with excitement because they're just promises with something extraordinary on the other side. We can surround ourselves with energizing people. Work can be enriching, dynamic and a rewarding part of our creative process. We can eliminate the space we give to negative emotions and fill our soul with love, hope, grace, generosity.

It requires faith to receive energy from God. He is the singular Source through which all of our vision for our future and healing can come. He is the confidence we need when we've been uncertain. He is our hope and courage when we're afraid. We we're never created to do life outside of Him. Jesus is the only one who can give us the unconditional love and energy that our soul longs for. We don't have all the answers. We need the love He came to give us.

We all have vision. Every one of us has a picture in our mind of our self, our family, our future. The questions are: What does your picture look like? Do you see yourself rising higher, overcoming obstacles, and living an abundant life? Or do you have a picture of yourself struggling, defeated, addicted, overweight and never getting good breaks? The pictures we allow in our mind will determine what kind of life we live. If our vision is limited, our life will be limited. The Scripture says that as a man thinks, so is he.

Before our dreams can come to pass, we have to see ourselves accomplishing the dreams. We have to get a picture of it. The pictures we keep in front of us—our vision—not only drop down into our spirit but get into our subconscious mind. Once something is subconscious, it will pull us toward it like gravity without is even thinking about it. If we will change these pictures and start seeing ourselves that way God sees us—blessed, prosperous, healthy, strong, talented and successful—instead of have something pulling against us, it will be pulling for us. We'll become magnets for God's power and move toward blessings, favor, promotion, and abundance.

God's dream for us is that we would be blessed in such a way that we could be a blessing to others. David said, "my cup runs over." God is an overflow God, but here's the key: we can't go around thinking thoughts of lack, not enough, struggle, and expect to have abundance. If we're going to become everything God has created us to be, we need to make up our minds to guard our energy and passionately pursue our transformation. We've got to be willing to un-become and unlearn who we became before we knew kingdom keys and principles and the things that the world taught us before we knew God. It's a rewiring.

We're being rewired to have the mind of Christ. We're being transformed by the renewing of our mind. The transformation doesn't come until the mind is renewed. We get renewed by the Word of God which is vastly different than the way the world thinks, believes and lives. The way we access the goodness of God is in coming up higher and looking ahead. It's not that the past didn't happen or that the pain wasn't real, but we don't live there anymore, and we refuse to reside in that dead place. We make up our minds that we're leaving the valley of dry bones, we're accessing he goodness of God and we're going to live lives that are full of destiny and purpose.

God often gives us formulas and things to work. For example, "I sought the Lord, and he answered me; he delivered me from all my fears" (Psalms 34:4). The key here is to seek the Lord and to become a person of the Word. This needs to be our firm stance and belief. The devil can't trigger us and tempt us as easily anymore. When the devil tries to start something, and we know the Scripture, can pull out a Word and the atmosphere must respond because God's Word doesn't return void. We don't just have to accept bad energy.

This is not something we're able to do ourselves. "Now to him who is able to do immeasurably more than all we ask or imagine, according to his power that is at work within us" (Ephesians 3:20). It's activating God's power in us that makes us powerful. There is a role for us to play. There is a job for us to do in this equation. The more we increase in our faith and position, the more God can release to us because we're able to handle more. More time in the Word will increase your faith. Commit to reading a chapter a day and watch what that does in your life. Ingesting the Word of God changes us. We literally are changed on a molecular level and our lives begin to come into alignment with kingdom order, kingdom thinking and kingdom living. The Word of God is transformational. It will increase our faith and increase our capacity and what God is able to release to us. It's a partnership and it's time to increase your faith, position, and the power that you walk in.

Activation: If someone could transcribe all your thoughts on paper, what would your thoughts spell out? Are your thoughts filled with problems and stressors? Are your thoughts rooted in poverty? If our thoughts are focused on all the things that keep us stuck; we can pretty much count on staying where we are. What we focus on expands in our lives. When we give out attention to something, we are tuning into and subscribing to it. We are designed to be magnets for God's power. Are you? Sometimes, we busy ourselves in other things or we're involved in things that we're not designed to be, and they drain us.

Make a list below of what drains you and what energizes you:

THINGS THAT DRAIN ME:	THINGS THAT ENERGIZE ME:

What are your takeaways with this activation?

Are you allowing God to energize you?

What are your next steps?

This week: Practice breaking through your obstacles. Usually, these obstacles are in our minds. Challenges yourself to shift your thinking to whatsoever is pure, lovely, noble and praiseworthy. Active the joy of the Lord that is your strength and take a brave bold step forward.

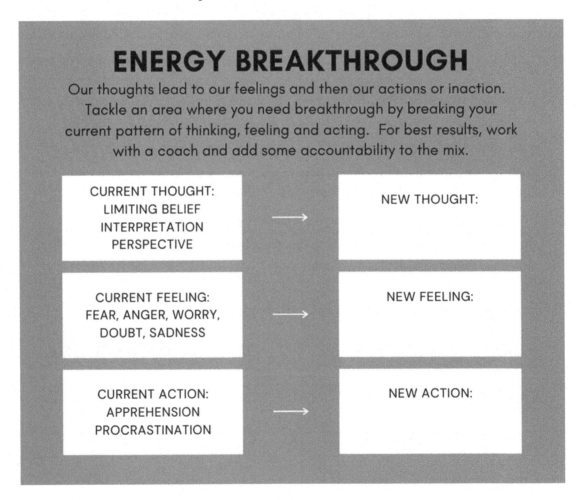

ENERGY BREAKTHROUGH

Our thoughts lead to our feelings and then our actions or inaction. Tackle an area where you need breakthrough by breaking your current pattern of thinking, feeling and acting. For best results, work with a coach and add some accountability to the mix.

CURRENT THOUGHT: LIMITING BELIEF INTERPRETATION PERSPECTIVE	→	NEW THOUGHT:
CURRENT FEELING: FEAR, ANGER, WORRY, DOUBT, SADNESS	→	NEW FEELING:
CURRENT ACTION: APPREHENSION PROCRASTINATION	→	NEW ACTION:

Use the diagram above to work through an area where you may be engaging in some stinking thinking, moody or straight up procrastination. Use your authority. What does the Word say about how to think, feel and act? Feel free to draw a column down a blank sheet of paper and work through as many shifts as you need.

EVALUATE YOUR VALUES

Whoever walks in integrity walks securely, but he who
makes his ways crooked will be found out.

—Proverbs 10:9 ESV

We can be a part of the exact same experience with someone and experience something at the exact same time and yet we have completely different perceptions and reactions to it. Have you noticed? Why is that? It's because of what we value. What we receive from an experience is a direct reflection of what we value. This is true with children as well. Two children can be raised in the same household and go in two completely different directions based on what they value and appreciate. Perceiving value is significant. It seems simplistic, but it's very important. In an often-overlooked passage of Scripture, Mary and Martha perceived a moment with Jesus totally different:

> She had a sister called Mary, who sat at the Lord's feet listening to what he said. But Martha was distracted by all the preparations that had to be made. She came to him and asked, "Lord, don't you care that my sister has left me to do the work by myself? Tell her to help me!"
>
> "Martha, Martha," the Lord answered, "you are worried and upset about many things, but few things are needed—or indeed only one. Mary has chosen what is better, and it will not be taken away from her (Luke 10:39-42 NIV).

Reflect on this moment. Mary and Martha have Jesus in their house. He was physically manifested in their house and Martha was worried about doing the dishes. She didn't see that she was missing out on a moment with Jesus. There are many Martha's in the world doing great work, but they've lost sight of Jesus. They may be doing good things, but they don't really value Jesus. Mary was focused on something completely different.

In this story, it doesn't look like Mary is giving anything and it seems like Martha is giving everything. Mary is giving something too, but it's not visible. She was giving her attention. Whatever we give our attention to is what we value. We suffer for lack of knowledge around what to value (see Hosea 4:6). When we want something for nothing we always fail. We may get by for a while but ultimately, we'll fail because there is a system in the earth of sowing and reaping and seed time and harvest. What we sow, we shall reap.

We need to be able to choose the best things to give for the moments we have. Martha has a moment with Jesus, but her values are not in the right place. It will always come back to haunt us when our values aren't in the right place. Notice, religion does the dishes; relationship sits at His feet. Here it is clear that Jesus values Mary's attention more than He does Martha's serving. What is God saying? When His Presence comes into the room, pay attention, don't be distracted. When we focus on something, we value it.

When I was first learning about the prophetic, I decided to register for what I call an immersion experience, where I could plant myself in a prophetic culture for a few days and see what it was all about. Conveniently there was literally one event that came up in my Google search results for the time I could travel, and it was a prophetic leadership conference. Coincidence? I had no idea what I was registering for but before I could overthink it, I registered.

I became more and more excited as the conference drew near and just days before it was postponed due to hurricane season and an unpredictable hurricane heading toward the state. I knew I'd heard God on going to the conference so rather than accepting a refund, I decided to wait it out and lean into what I was choosing to believe as divine timing. The conference was scheduled for six months later. This was divine timing as it served to intensify my hunger to learn and grow in the kingdom. This was also when I penned my second book *God's Vibes Matter: Co-Laboring with God*.

As I traveled across the country, I had an expectant heart. While I was in a foreign environment, meeting new people and stepping out of my grid of what I was accustomed to, things strangely made sense. On the last day of the conference, we were told we were going to receive a prophetic word from one of the ministry team members. This was the first prophetic word that I received. The woman that released the word was lovely and I remember the experience clearly especially the part where she broke down the challenge of discerning when to be Mary and when to be Martha.

I didn't know what to expect, but I think a part of me was hoping for some good news, a confirmation or something that would amp me up to go back home. This was that word and I'm glad I recorded it so that I could unpack it and discover that later. I hadn't studied this Mary and Martha story, but my old man nature was quite fond of living like Martha, while my new creation self was really starting to vibe with Mary. I could see how this is always an inner wrestle, when to be still and when to move. What I found is that we live in a fear of missing out culture where we're applauded for doing all the things, but it's Who we know and spend time with that changes everything. I was being led to strengthen my roots in God so that I could face one of the most challenging seasons of my life. Like Martha, I needed to see the real treasure that Mary knew in simply being with Jesus.

Martha could not see that the real treasure of the moment was to get to sit at the feet of Jesus who wasn't going to be there very long. The needless things that were on her mind were not important. She wanted to make Mary get up and enter her lower valuation of Jesus. Mary had chosen the good part.

There is a correlation between valuing time with God and the miraculous power of God being exemplified in our lives. In other words, we don't waste time when we give Jesus our time and attention. Every praise, worship, moment of meditation, devotion, consecration, conversation with Him while driving to work, all comes back to bless us in a time of need or grief to strengthen us in a way that we would not be strengthened had we not had a relationship with Him. Think about it this way. Have you ever had people come to you without a real relationship with you and ask for you to do things for them? No one wants to open the door to a request, but to a friend. After the friendship has been established then we can listen to a request and we'll hear it differently when we know that our friend knocked on the door for us and not just for the request.

Some of the greatest things that happen to us, we don't fully value at the time. Out of all the things on the list that need to be done, what is the one thing that is priority? We need be clear on what we value most so that we can simplify to amplify. To refine our priorities, we must evaluate our core values. Is it loyalty, trust, integrity, companionship? What would you leave dirty dishes to have?

Jesus was offering Martha the chance to have a relationship that ultimately would save her brother Lazarus's life. What we do with a moment like this determines what's destined. Whatever we value before we need it, is what comes back to bless us when we need it. Here are some things to consider when it comes to evaluating our values:

1. Beware of the danger of inflation-We need to be careful not to think of ourselves more highly than we ought. It's a dangerous thing to have an overinflated self-image.
2. Don't settle for deflation-Just because someone else has a lower value of us, that doesn't mean that's how we should see ourselves. When we have a low value of ourselves, we tend to surround ourselves with people that don't honor and respect us.
3. Our credit card reflects our values-What we value we give money and attention to. Are you asking God to value you with what He has to give you, while you don't value Him with what you have to give Him? What changes do you need to make in what you give to and pay attention to change the outcome of your life?
4. Value is more than dollars-It's time and attention.
5. Value begins with childhood experiences-How we value ourselves has a lot to do with things that happened or didn't happen to us when we were children. The feeling of self-worth starts with children. When we don't train up a child in the way they should go,

life teaches them. We must be born again and start with fresh experiences and a fresh identity. We can build our hopes on things that are eternal that correct the appraisal we should have received.

6. Re-evaluate through upgrades-Upgrades in the spirit lead to upgrades in the natural. We can always upgrade our intimacy, renewed thoughts, wise words, spirit-ed actions, abundant beliefs, bold faith, and authority.

Read this verse:

Each one should test their own actions. Then they can take pride in themselves alone, without comparing themselves to someone else, for each one should carry their own load. Nevertheless, the one who receives instruction in the word should share all good things with their instructor.

Do not be deceived: God cannot be mocked. A man reaps what he sows. Whoever sows to please their flesh, from the flesh will reap destruction; whoever sows to please the Spirit, from the Spirit will reap eternal life. Let us not become weary in doing good, for at the proper time we will reap a harvest if we do not give up. Therefore, as we have opportunity, let us do good to all people, especially to those who belong to the family of believers (Galatians 6:4-10).

Each of us should test our own actions. That's where self-esteem and self-respect come from when we can carry our own load. What are you valuing? Where's your evidence? Is your life being transformed by the miraculous working power of the living God? One of the way's you'll know if you're being transformed is ff you're getting new courage in hard times, being stabilized in storms, and strengthened in crisis.

Get the Word in you and let it do what it's designed to do. Let it transform, kill, correct, resurrect, restore, and upgrade you. That's the one thing that will increase your value. You're a designer's original and you're designed to bring forth much fruit. God-worth is about getting values in the right place and life is all about values.

Reminder: Distractions take us off course and often pull us away from values. Guard against this and start simply by developing a morning routine. It's a must to start the day with peace. What would happen if the very first thing you did was give thanks to God and sit with your thoughts? What if you made it a practice to pray, read, meditate on scriptures, and work out before you show up and serve anything or anyone else? When you give yourself the quality time with God, love, attention, care, and affirmation that you need to operate as your best self, then you can serve others from an overflowing cup. What would happen if you made it a habit to keep yourself all filled up so that you could serve people as inspired from your overflow? Leave room for God's Presence in your life.

Activation: Conscious values allow you to take positive action. They are "want to's." Use the Values Assessment Tool as a starting point to help you clarify your Top 5 Values.

Rate each value on a scale of 1 to 10 based on its importance in your life. Then rate each value on a scale of 1 to 10 based on how well you live each value and "walk the talk."

VALUE	VALUE RATING: 1-10	ACTION RATING: 1-10
ACCOMPLISHMENT		
ABUNDANCE		
ACHIEVEMENT		
ADVENTURE		
AUTONOMY		
BEAUTY		
CLARITY		
COMMITMENT		
COMMUNICATION		
COMMUNITY		
CONNECTING TO OTHERS		
CREATIVITY		
EMOTIONAL HEALTH		
ENVIRONMENT		
EXCELLENCE		
FAMILY		
FLEXIBILITY		
FREEDOM		
FRIENDSHIP		
FULFILLMENT		
FUN		

HOLISTIC LIVING		
HONESTY		
HUMOR		
INTEGRITY		
INTIMACY		
JOY		
LEADERSHIP		
LOYALTY		
NATURE		
OPENNESS		
ORDERLINESS		
PERSONAL GROWTH		
PARTNERSHIP		
PHYSICAL APPEARANCE		
POWER		
PRIVACY		
PROFESSIONALISM		
RECOGNITION		
RESPECT		
ROMANCE		
SECURITY		
SELF-CARE		
SELF-EXPRESSION		
SELF-MASTERY		
SELF-REALIZATION		
SENSUALITY		
SERVICE		
SPIRITUALITY		
TRUST		
TRUTH		
VITALITY		
WALKING THE TALK		

This Week: List your Top 5 Values and WHY these are important to you. Reference the Daily 5 to Thrive Checklist below. What are 5 actions that you can take daily to embody what you value and walk your talk?

DAILY 5

CHECKLIST

- ✓ Quiet Time-15-60 minutes of prayer, study, meditation, reading or journaling.

- ✓ Move your body-30-60 minutes. Release stress, build strength and self-discipline.

- ✓ Drink Water and Eat Clean-Is this energizing me and nourishing my body?

- ✓ Sow and Serve-Blessed to be a blessing. Is this what I want to see a harvest of?

- ✓ Gratitude-What am I grateful for? What are my top 3 wins for the day?

- ✓ Bonus: How did God move today?

#godsvibesmatter
www.julianapage.com

PAY THE PRICE

The Lord is not slow in keeping his promise, as some understand
slowness. Instead he is patient with you, not wanting anyone
to perish, but everyone to come to repentance.

—2 Peter 2:9 NIV

So many of us say that we want to change, but many of us are unwilling to pay the price to change. All of change comes from focusing on what we can control, not focusing on what we can't control, and all change has a price tag attached to it. We have to count the cost. Do we actually want to change? Are we willing to pay the price for change?

Jesus over and over again has a bold and blatant message. He makes it very clear that following Him comes with an extreme cost. He says things like if you want to follow me, you have to deny yourself and take up your cross. One time He says, unless you eat my flesh and drink my blood, you have no life in you. Jesus did not sugar coat His message. He wanted us to understand that yes salvation is free, but it isn't cheap.

In Jesus there is a brand-new creation at hand and because of Jesus we can change, and we can become who we've been called to become. We can have a free relationship with God through the Son. Jesus is not just a man; He is God in the flesh. When Jesus is revealed on the earth, the beauty of divinity is followed by the brutality of humanity. In the Gospel of Mark, God's Son is about to meet God's adversary. "At once the Spirit sent him out into the wilderness, and he was in the wilderness forty days, being tempted by Satan. He was with the wild animals, and angels attended him" (Mark 1:12-13 NIV).

The same Spirit that descended upon Jesus in one moment then sends Him out into the desert. Public declaration will always face private temptation. A lot of times we are fond of the idea of being led by the Spirit and most of us think that when we're being led by the Spirit, He's going to lead us to breakthrough, success, healing, and prosperity. He does lead us to those places but for those that want to change and grow that comes with being led into the wilderness. Will you obey the Spirit when He sends you into the desert?

It's only in the desert where we can truly appreciate water because the desert is a place that makes us desperate. It's desperation for God that creates revelation about God. The wilderness is not a great place to build a home, but it is a great place to build our faith. If we want to change, we have to be willing to have these wilderness experiences with our Maker.

Jesus was being led into the desert to be tempted by Satan. All of us on the journey of faith will have to go through these experiences where we feel like we're in the wilderness, but we'll move differently when we recognize that the desert is meant to make us desperate for God. What happens to so many of us is that in the wilderness, we fail to learn how to pass the test of temptation. If we could get this revelation, we'd find ourselves being more content on the faith journey.

When I decided to give my life to Christ, it was out of desperation. I desperately needed my life to change, and I felt powerless to bring about that change in my own strength and understanding. While I mostly wanted things on the outside to change, I inherently knew the change would be on my insides too, I just didn't accurately assess just how big those changes would be.

I desired to grow closer to God, so I decided to get re-baptized. I'd technically been baptized as a baby, but I wanted to demonstrate my commitment and faith as an adult with my whole heart behind it. While it was significant, it seemed like the following weeks were filled with challenges and attacks that I didn't see coming. Some part of me felt like things would get easier, at least within the first week. They didn't get easier, they got real. Now my focus, decision-making, character, and capacity were being challenged. I said I wanted this new life, was I willing to walk out the newness of life that required changing details of my life as I knew them?

So many of us make a new public declaration of being a new creation in Christ and then the moment we make that declaration, we all the sudden face deeper, bigger, greater temptation. Many times, our public victories are followed by our greatest private attacks. We go from being a trend to becoming a threat. We go from being a spectator to becoming a participant. We will never change if we can't afford to stop feeding our flesh. Wanting to change is not enough. On the side-lines we don't get tackled. Disobedience is the best way to delay our destiny. Being willing to resist temptation on the journey is the only way we'll continue to become. We'll have to conquer the test of temptation if we're going to see the result God has for our lives. It's our obedience that leads to life and life more abundantly.

A lot of us want to follow God as long as it leads to our success. Success ended up being on a cross for Jesus and it ended up in a prison cell for John the Baptist. "After John was put in prison, Jesus went into Galilee, proclaiming the good news of God. "The time has come," he said. "The kingdom of God has come near. Repent and believe the good news" (Mark 1:14-15)! Growth and change through steps of obedience don't always lead to the life we were thinking that we wanted but they always lead to the life that we needed.

Today is the most valuable thing we have to give. Oscar Wilde said, "These days everyone knows the price of everything and the value of nothing." If we want to know the price of what change is, it's the cost of today. Change happens in a moment; it's results that require time. We spend more time on excuses than we do on execution. Jesus said that the time is right now to believe the good news. Salvation isn't a tomorrow thing. Jesus is here right now. It might look like an ordinary day to everyone else, but it could be our most extraordinary day. Tomorrow is not promised, and this life is but a vapor.

Jesus looked for loyalty over everything. "As Jesus walked beside the Sea of Galilee, he saw Simon and his brother Andrew casting a net into the lake, for they were fishermen. "Come, follow me," Jesus said, "and I will send you out to fish for people." At once they left their nets and followed him. When he had gone a little farther, he saw James son of Zebedee and his brother John in a boat, preparing their nets. Without delay he called them, and they left their father Zebedee in the boat with the hired men and followed him" (Mark 1:16-20).

Believers believe but disciples do. Disciple means an apprentice of a teacher, learning the ways of Jesus. We walk, think, talk, do like Jesus. Loyalty is proved in what we're willing to lose not what we're hoping to gain. The cost of moving from a career to a calling for example, is everything. Jesus is not calling us to hate actively, he's calling us to hate comparatively. Loyalty to Jesus looks like following Him and loving Him with such diligence and endurance that every other earthly attachment compared to that love looks like hate. He must be the goal, our finish line, and the prize. The cost of change is putting God at the center and orbiting around Him.

> Suppose one of you wants to build a tower. Won't you first sit down and estimate the cost to see if you have enough money to complete it? For if you lay the foundation and are not able to finish it, everyone who sees it will ridicule you, saying, 'This person began to build and wasn't able to finish.' "Or suppose a king is about to go to war against another king. Won't he first sit down and consider whether he is able with ten thousand men to oppose the one coming against him with twenty thousand? If he is not able, he will send a delegation while the other is still a long way off and will ask for terms of peace. In the same way, those of you who do not give up everything you have cannot be my disciples (Luke 14:28-33 NIV).

We need to weigh the cost and give up everything if we're going after the kingdom and desire to rule and reign in life. We can change when we surrender to who God is and His plan. We don't have enough willpower to change, we must surrender to the good He has in store for us. Are you willing and obedient (see Isaiah 1:19-20)?

Activation: Sometimes the choices we make, or don't make, limit your potential. Other times, you don't even see the choices that you have. Both are often rooted in energy blocks that hold you back from your potential. Look at the energy block chart and answer the questions below.

Energy Blocks That Prevent Change

LIMITING BELIEFS

LIMITING BELIEFS ARE THINGS WE ACCEPT ABOUT LIFE, ABOUT OURSELVES, ABOUT OUR WORLD, OR ABOUT PEOPLE THAT LIMIT US IN SOME WAY.

INTERPRETATIONS

AN INTERPRETATION IS AN OPINION OR JUDGEMENT THAT WE CREATE ABOUT AN EVENT, SITUATION, PERSON, OR EXPERIENCE AND BELIEVE TO BE TRUE.

INNER CRITIC

OUR INNER CRITIC IS AN INNER VOICE THAT TELLS US THAT IN ONE WAY OR ANOTHER, WE'RE NOT GOOD ENOUGH.

ASSUMPTIONS

AN ASSUMPTION IS AN EXPECTATION THAT, BECAUSE SOMETHING HAS HAPPENED IN THE PAST, IT WILL HAPPEN AGAIN.

1. List some of the beliefs that you have that don't line up with the Word of God and may be limiting you in some way:

2. Next to each belief, write out a new belief that can replace it and visualize the new potential you can step into.

3. What are some of the assumptions you make that hold you back?

4. Challenge the assumptions you listed with this question: Just because that happened in the past, why must it happen again?

5. What are some of the interpretations you've made up to explain current or recent situations in your life? How have your interpretations affected you and others?

6. What is God's point of view on the situations you listed?

7. What messages have you been hearing from your inner critic?

8. Decide on something to say to your inner critic when he/she shows up. Keep refining what you say until you come up with something that feels good and allows you to move forward.

This Week: Think about what you would like to change in your life. A behavior? An emotion? A feeling? An attitude? A mindset?

What feelings come up when you think of obedience? Reframe obedience to the gifts and possibilities that are in it.

Think of a time you did not obey what you thought God was telling you. What were the consequences? How can you avoid falling into the same thing again?

Think of a time you obeyed God. What was the fruit of that obedience in your life?

What are two decisions you made in the past that have positively shaped your life? How did they change your life for the better? What finally got you to decide?

What are two new decisions you are committed to making now, and how will they powerfully improve your life forever?

PURSUE GOD'S WILL

Your kingdom come, your will be done, on earth as it is in heaven.

—Matthew 6:10 NIV

*O*ur expectations set the limits for our lives. If we expect little, we're going to receive little. Our expectations are our faith at work. Many times, we're told not to have expectations and then we won't be disappointed. While it's true that our expectations work in both directions, positive and negative and we draw those things in, if we don't have expectations then we're not releasing our faith. Our faith needs a job, and we need to develop an undeniable quality of expecting good things. We need to remain passionate and excited about something. David said in Psalms: "Surely goodness and mercy will follow me all the days of my life." Is that what you're expecting?

Not only does negativity tend to take up more space in our minds, but the devil also wants to take up space by throwing lies and helping us look for the next disaster, failure, or bad break. Knowing this, we have to be proactive in pursuing God and the kingdom which is defined as righteousness, peace and joy in the Holy Spirit (see Romans 14:17). It's all about how we train our minds and what we train ourselves to focus on and align with. God is looking for us to be full of faith and full of the Holy Spirit. Our journey to rule and reign in life isn't a behavioral improvement program, it's an ever-evolving relationship with God where we increase in our knowledge of Him as we pursue knowing Him. As we focus on His greatness, we draw it into our lives. As we trust His leading and develop a track record with Him, our faith increases to do the greater works Jesus promised we'd do (see John 14:12). The Apostle Paul said it this way:

> [For my determined purpose is] that I may know Him [that I may progressively become more deeply and intimately acquainted with Him, perceiving and recognizing and understanding the wonders of His Person more strongly and more clearly], and that I may in that same way come to know the power outflowing from His resurrection [which it exerts over believers], and that I may so share His sufferings as to be continually transformed [in spirit into His likeness even] to His death, [in the hope]" (Philippians 3:10 AMPC).

Pursuing God is about upgrading our expectations and our faith settings around what we believe is possible, and we do this when we make it our purpose and priority to know Him. As we pursue Him through relationship, we focus on Him and what He says in His Word, how He moves through characters in the Bible and through His spirit in and around us. Through our focus on Him, we draw more of Him and His kingdom into our lives and we discover that we're not only being transformed into His likeness, but we're empowered by His Spirit to walk in greater power and authority. It's not our might or strength, but His Spirit.

Pursuing God and His will is important because it's not only God's requirement, but when this isn't our priority, we shift from ruling and reigning in life to allowing other things to rule and reign over us. It's the attitude of our hearts and minds that God is after. As God's representatives, we can help others enjoy what Jesus died for us to have. We can help restore them to the knowledge of god and His love for them, but we can't do this when we don't know Him for ourselves or when we're caught up in other things. We strive to give God what He truly requires, which is to do what is just, love mercy and kindness and walk humbly with Him (see Micah 6:8).

Our pursuit of God is something that is tested for its authenticity, purity, and depth. Are we only pursuing God to get His gifts and what He has to give us? Abraham's story provides a great example of his pursuit, heart attitude and mind attitude being tested. Read this excerpt of his test:

> Some time later God tested Abraham. He said to him, "Abraham!"
> "Here I am," he replied.
>
> Then God said, "Take your son, your only son, whom you love—Isaac—and go to the region of Moriah. Sacrifice him there as a burnt offering on a mountain I will show you."
>
> Early the next morning Abraham got up and loaded his donkey. He took with him two of his servants and his son Isaac. When he had cut enough wood for the burnt offering, he set out for the place God had told him about. On the third day Abraham looked up and saw the place in the distance. He said to his servants, "Stay here with the donkey while I and the boy go over there. We will worship and then we will come back to you."
>
> Abraham took the wood for the burnt offering and placed it on his son Isaac, and he himself carried the fire and the knife. As the two of them went on together, Isaac spoke up and said to his father Abraham, "Father?"
>
> "Yes, my son?" Abraham replied.
> "The fire and wood are here," Isaac said, "but where is the lamb for the burnt offering?"

Abraham answered, "God himself will provide the lamb for the burnt offering, my son." And the two of them went on together.

When they reached the place God had told him about, Abraham built an altar there and arranged the wood on it. He bound his son Isaac and laid him on the altar, on top of the wood. Then he reached out his hand and took the knife to slay his son. But the angel of the Lord called out to him from heaven, "Abraham! Abraham!" "Here I am," he replied.

"Do not lay a hand on the boy," he said. "Do not do anything to him. Now I know that you fear God, because you have not withheld from me your son, your only son."

Abraham looked up and there in a thicket he saw a ram caught by its horns. He went over and took the ram and sacrificed it as a burnt offering instead of his son. So Abraham called that place The Lord Will Provide. And to this day it is said, "On the mountain of the Lord it will be provided" (Genesis 22:1-14 NIV).

Abraham passed the test because He knew one thing, the Giver comes first. As far as Abraham was concerned, God was talking crazy talk from his point of view. For us that would be like God talking to someone about buying a house when they're late on rent or talking to someone else about starting a business when they just lost a job. God talk is crazy talk. God says things that don't make sense. We walk in our senses much of the time and report the news or what is happening or what hasn't happened yet even when we're told to walk in our spirit and by faith. God talks to Abraham about having a child while he was barren. Can you imagine if God said that to you?

Pursuing God is determining that we will not lose our faith and confidence or our connection with Him. We must constantly pursue God and actively wait on Him for His wisdom and direction. Abraham waits 100 years. At the most impossible time, God fulfills His promise to him. If it had not been for the Lord, it wouldn't have happened. Abraham was told to go to Moriah which was a string of mountains and yet he was never told what one. Abraham didn't ask God how he would know, he trusted if he got in the region, God would show him. His crazy faith met God's crazy talk.

We can't walk with God if we always have to see the way clear. Like Abraham, if we get in the region, God will show us everything we need to know. We need to get closer to what we're praying for and expecting God to do. He won't tell us in advance, but when we get in the region,

He'll show us. That could mean getting around the people, doing research to find the place, or finding a mentor in a specific industry.

Pursuing God is the most amazing mission of our lives. If we really start following Him, He will scare us to death and take us to places we never expected to go and do things we never expected to do. It's stories like Abraham's that make us afraid of what we're going to lose when we pursue the Lord. Like Abraham we will have to put everything on the line. Isaac to Abraham, represented access to everything God had ever done in his life. He had to have an Isaac because God promised him that through his seed all nations shall be blessed. Imagine what must have been running through his mind as he was riding up a hill to kill his promise. Isaac is the promise. What has God promised you? What are you willing to sacrifice to see it happen?

One of the most difficult things for me to sacrifice was my coaching business. It made absolutely no logical sense. It had taken years to discover the calling, not to mention, I'd poured all of my savings into training when this could have been a down payment for my first home. I wrestled pursuing coaching while finishing my graduate degree, but I had such a strong knowing that I had to, which was a huge risk at the time. After graduating graduate school and completing my coaching certification and advanced certifications, I moved across the country to go to the "place" that God had shown me.

As I settled into that place, launched the coaching business, and started doing well, I felt that knowing again in my spirit. I was being led to kill the business. How could this be? This was everything that God had shown me. I was doing what I thought we're all the right and aligned things and I was supposed to just stop with no other options? It was a brutal way of asking, "do you trust Me?" I didn't have a back-up plan, I was on my own in this new place, without family and friends so I really felt like I might be crazy. Even so, I knew what I knew. If I continued when I was given this clear directive, things would have only become more difficult. So, I obeyed. I deleted the website and all traces of the business on the internet, moved out of my office and waited for my next directive. I didn't know that God would bring coaching back around in a greater way, I thought that was it.

Finding the right place when pursuing God is so important. The ability to discern when you are in the right place is the most important gift you can have because His promises won't work out of place. Many times, God doesn't give us a GPS, address, map or description. He says we'll know it when we see it. We'll have no direction, all we'll have is the instinct that we'll know it when we see it. Real pursuit always includes sacrifice. We can live in the "I'm not there yet but I see it" place for far longer than we want to. There is a place in the spirit that we need to fight our way into. It's the place where God can do what He's trying to do in our lives.

"God is a Spirit: and they that worship him must worship him in spirit and in truth" (John 4:24 KJV). There is a place in the spirit where miracles happen. There is a place in the spirit where no confusion will dwell, where the pain will dissipate, where wellness will come to the mind, where no weapon formed shall be able to prosper, where provision is released. We have to go for this place in the spirit alone.

The closer we get to the place, the more we separate from people. When we find the place, we can't take everyone with us. We can slow down our journey when people that don't have the same hunger to the glory. The place is where the miracles happen. The place expedites the journey. There are some people that God has anointed to walk us into the place He has for us and we don't want to go on with anyone that isn't designed to because we have too much on the line.

When Abraham was about to slay his son, that was the moment where God knew he could give him a gift and it wouldn't be an idol. He'd finally came to a place where it wasn't about the gift but about the giver. God needs to know He can give us something without it replacing Him. He'll give us desires if they don't become our god. Every now and again He will test us to make sure that He will always come first. Will you let something separate you from the love of God? Is He worth more than what He gives? What God has for us no one else can get, but we must pursue God to get it. When He knows He comes first, He knows we're ready to get it.

If Abraham had gone up any other mountain, any other mountain would have killed his son. This was only one mountain where the ram was provided. God already had provision for Abraham, He was just waiting on Him to find the place. The name of place the was called Jehovah Jireh. There is a place for each of us that is our Jehovah Jireh, where our rams can't get away, and no one can have our promises. We are not waiting on the promise, the place or the provision, they're waiting on you. Are you bold enough to believe that there is a ram tied up in the thicket for every circumstance in your life? There is no doubt, the only unknown is finding the place. What is your ram? Is it salvation, peace or wholeness? What do you need to loose your ram? Is it a deeper consecration? Is there anyone you need to let go?

Pursuing God's will is empowering. Empowerment is awareness of God and His guidance in the moment. Many folks would like to have a 1-day relationship with God and become sloppy thinkers. Relationship is daily. It's often when something happens that is very painful, that we decide to gain control over own thoughts. When we walk by faith, we don't have to accept what we see or what is as reality. We create and walk by faith. We can get to a place where we're hard-wired for alignment with God. Life will reveal opportunities for us to come back into alignment constantly. It's a blessing to have a home base and one that wants us to live well. When we split our energy, we make room for confusion and double mindedness. We can practice living in alignment daily. We're in control of our own experience. When we take control of our experience and start our day with God, we begin to notice how our lives unfold with grace.

When we pinch ourselves off from God and our supernatural resources it begins to manifest in our realities in all sorts of different ways. We don't have to keep telling those stories of keeping that momentum going. Often, we're not joyful because we're trying to navigate without the Holy Spirit and our guidance. We need life to help us focus. When we have experience that points us toward what we want, that's a beautiful thing because it helps us to focus. Our pursuit is not about getting anywhere it's about going somewhere with God. Because we are eternal, joy-seeking beings, we keep finding opportunities to expand. That's what it's all about, it's an ongoing exploration of joyful life experience. We don't create to get it done, we create because we're creators and because creating is a joyful experience. We know what we don't want, we know what we do want, we realize we're not a match to what we do want and we go deeper with God to align with and increase our capacity to expand into the more that He has for us. We focus and we discern with our spirit, and we shift, and we maintain this alignment and we come to believe and expect and then we close the gap and for just a moment, there is a glorious satisfying, culmination and manifestation which then provide another set of experiences. The pursuit of God continues because there is always deeper that we can go with Him.

It's never about how much is created, what we're creating in comparison with anyone else, it's only what we allow life to produce for us in terms of our desires and our willingness to line up with that. Just the fulfilment of coming into alignment with God each day is a joyful thing. When we sync up with God, we become empowered and simultaneously sync up with everything that He has for us. We begin to feel His invincibility and our powerful partnership with Him. It's the partnership where our clarity, enthusiasm and authority flow. We feel completely our worthiness and we know what it really means to be alive. It's mastery of life experience and nothing else will do. Once we catch this, we have no interest to compare with others, because we only desire to close the gap between where we are and where God is leading and by discipline hold ourselves in sync with Him and that.

It pales in comparison to worldly success. It's us getting up to speed with our expansion. If we don't get up to speed, we don't feel good. When we do get up to speed there aren't words to describe how good that feels. There are no dry seasons in Christ. Alignment isn't like a college degree where once we achieve it, it's ours forevermore. It either is or it isn't in the moment and that's a beautiful thing. We discern it and find it and we wouldn't be able to do that if life didn't present us with opportunities and the contrast to. It's not about beating ourselves up for not being aligned, it's pursuing consistent alignment.

Jesus said in John 4:14, "but whoever drinks of the water that I will give him, he will never by thirsty again. The water that I will give him will become in him a spring of water welling up to eternal life." Dryness is not on His end. If we find ourselves in the proximity of a dry land, then we should just make it a place of springs as in Psalms 84:6, "As they go through the Valley of Baca they make it a place of springs; the early rain also covers it with pools." He has provided so much living water that it will come out of us if we would just believe. Being aligned with

God is empowerment and a steady acknowledgement of Who God is and who we are through Christ. It's that steadiness that we're reaching for in our lives. We have an intense desire for alignment that would not be there had we not experience life without Him. It's just a matter of following after Him with all of our heart and recalibrating along the way. That's being on the leading edge in life.

No one wants to hear that it's about the journey, but it is. We need to rest in God and stop taking score of where we are. When we care about alignment with Him only, the other things line up—seek the kingdom first. If we cared about that only, we'd value what we create and be intentional with our focus to produce spirit-led momentum. We would be more aware of when we're moving toward the fulfillment of who we are and when we're drifting from it. We become conscious, deliberate creators that are fueled by God and allow God to move in our lives. We appreciate Him more than anything. Our relationship is between us and God not us and the world. We're not trying to conquer and climb the highest mountain; we're trying to get to our place. We get better and better at being aligned every day.

Are you ready to start obeying God even if it doesn't make a lot of sense to you? Life can and should be a real adventure, if we really everyday say to God, "I'm available for You." We don't often get what we want the moment that we want it. God may have something big for us to do, but He often leads a longer path than we desire because we're not ready for the things God has for us. We don't grow up in our good times, we grow up in our hard times. We grow when it's inconvenient, uncomfortable, and when people aren't treating nice. We need to be willing to do things just because God said to do it. Everything God asks us to do, He does give us the grace to do it. We don't have to know why or when we're going to get a breakthrough. We only know that living in God's will and pursing God's will is the safest and most fruitful place to be. When we stop making excuses and become available for whatever God wants to do, then life becomes a real adventure.

Activation: We can enjoy being in tough places if we have the right attitude. List 3 fears that you currently have.

With each, practice the Three R's:

- Stop Rehearsing
- Release it
- Replace it

Fears don't go away on their own. When pursuing God, we'll face several fears which is why we're constantly encouraged to be bold and courageous. What

71

are practical actions that you can take to overcome your fears and adjust your faith setting?

For example, if you're afraid to do inner healing work that you've put off, maybe it's praying for God to guide you to the right therapist, researching online and signing up. Another example, maybe you're led to launch a business and you don't feel like you have the tools, perhaps it's registering in a business program or coaching. Maybe there is an addiction that you've been struggling and it's time to start a recovery program. Ask Holy Spirit what actions to take now to replace your fears?

This Week: Think about the word pursue. It means to follow, to seek to attain or accomplish a goal over a long period, or to continue to investigate, explore or discuss.

What have you been actively pursuing?

What has God given you the grace to pursue in this season?

What does it look like for you to pursue God?

Willpower becomes the willingness to accept God's power to guide your life. Check the spiritual base for your life with the acronym below.

Do I:

- **B**elieve Jesus Christ dies on the cross for me and shower He was God by coming back to life? (1 Corinthians 15:2-4)
- **A**ccept God's free forgiveness for my sins? (Romans 3:22)
- **S**witch to God's plan for my life? (Matthew 1:16, Romans 12:2)
- **E**xpress my desire for Christ to be the director of my life? (Romans 10:9)

If you are ready to take this step, pray this prayer out loud. If you have already taken this step, use this prayer to recommit and continue to seek and follow God's will.

Dear God, I believe you sent Your Son, Jesus, to die for my sins so I can be forgiven. I'm sorry for my sins, and I want to life the rest of my life the way You want me to. Please put Your Spirit in my life to direct me, Amen.

If you made the decision to invite Christ into your life, let someone know. Feel free to visit www.julianapage.com and send a testimony.

Part Three

RENEW YOUR MIND

So we do not lose heart. Though our outer self is wasting
away, our inner self is being renewed day by day.

—2 Corinthians 6:16 ESV

Unless we expect to see and hear from the unseen realm, then our experience will be limited to our limited expectations. In other words, our expectation will create the measure of our reception. Once we are able to admit that we have a spirit that is aware of and has knowledge about a realm that our brain cannot see or hear, then we will have made the first step in our journey of walking according to the spirit. God created the mind to serve us, not to keep us in captivity.

Changing what we believe about someone, or something will change the feelings attached to it. Under the influence of the Holy Spirit, we have the power to transform, fellowship with God and manifest the power of the Kingdom (see John 14:12). When we recognize that we are transformed by renewing out minds through reading and studding the Word of God, we become empowered with what we need to arise and shine as sent ones in the world (see Matthew 5:14, Isaiah 60:1, John 20:21).

"Finally, brothers and sisters, whatever is true, whatever is noble, whatever is right, whatever is pure, whatever is lovely, whatever is admirable—if anything is excellent or praiseworthy—think about such things" (Philippians 4:8 NIV) Many times we do the opposite of Philippians 4:8. We meditate on our failures and things are wrong or we think on things that inspire us into hopelessness or pain. Think of the brain not just as an organ for thinking, but as a radio receiver that picks up different stations (according to what the receiver is tuned to). When we are focused on and tuned into the enemy's station, we hear an inner voice tell us how inadequate, unimportant, and unlovable we are. Our imaginations then build proofed that these thoughts are true. Eventually, thoughts that we continually tune into will become our own beliefs, not just passing thoughts.

Just as we question which thoughts are of God and which are our own, we should consider whether thoughts are the enemy's or ours. More importantly, we should be thinking on purpose as Philippians 4:8 says, rather than being victims of the airwaves. To think on purpose means that we are not just playing defense and rejecting negative thoughts, but we are on the offense and purposely deciding what we want to think about.

When we pursue God's will through His Word, we'll be challenged to manifest what's at our core for us to really adjust our crown. Our crown is our energetic makeup, our vibe, or our frequency (thoughts, words, actions, moods, attitudes). This is why God's Vibes Matter. The way God thinks, how He moves, how He encounters us, how He speaks, how He guides and correct all teach us how to tune into Him and walk in obedience. Our vibes are what we currently are at our core. This doesn't always align with God, so the tuning process is constant. We must tap into God's strength to actually tune into His will, transform and then occupy the throne as He intended.

We'll have to tap into the self-initiative and the courage and boldness to be a king or a queen without apologizing to anyone or seeking anyone's approval. We'll have to step into fears and walk in greatness even if the world disapproves. We'll be challenged to control our emotions and intentionally conquer them. We'll intentionally mature in our ability and capacity to dictate the atmospheres around us. We'll fill our mind with the Word of God to uproot strongholds and self-correct immediately. We'll throw down inferiority and claim our royalty authentically and in a sustainable way. We'll connect with our authentic selves and live our true value and God's original intention. We'll actualize power, potential and giftings as individuals. As we rule and reign over ourselves and our assignments, we'll find our true source of fulfillment and we begin stepping into the fullness of our power and guiding humanity into a brighter future.

Renewing our minds is often confronting things. We can't get comfortable hiding from our stuff. It teaches us to redirect our focus to the things that are within. It's knowing ourselves from our core. It's owning our destiny and expanding in our purpose. It's having the faith in ourselves to step into our future even if we have to go alone. It will demand we conquer ignorance, insecurity, lethargy and lack of initiative.

There's a lot of things we'll have to do afraid. When we're afraid of something that's when we need to run to it because if we don't, we'll be running from it the rest of our lives. To get to our core, we must heal emotionally from the trauma of our history and experiences. The trauma tries to prevent our future. We have to think about what we're thinking and purge the poison of the propaganda that has only served to limit us. The good news is, the more we pour truth into ourselves, the lies will rise to the top, spill over and go down the drain. We have to get uncomfortable and begin to manifest our true greatness.

As we develop our spiritual senses as opposed to just our logic or physical senses, we'll grow in wisdom and discernment and be able to recognize and perceive the subtleties of God. In the world for example, we might hear something like, faith is calculated, favor is networking and friendship is strategic, however the Word says something different.

1. Faith is not calculated. Faith is a byproduct of intimacy, and it comes as a response to the voice of God. We can't work it up, make it up, or even fake it until we make it. It is not a series of careful calculations or a result of playing the odds. It is the visible evidence of our invisible hope that is anchored in Christ alone.

   "Now faith is the substance of things hoped for, the evidence of things not seen" (Hebrews 11:1).

   "This *hope* we have as an anchor of the soul, both sure and steadfast, and which enters the *Presence* behind the veil, here the forerunner has entered for us, *even* Jesus, having become High Priest forever according to the order of Melchizedek" (Hebrews 6:19-20 NKJV).

2. Favor is not networking. Favor is a shield attained through righteousness as we walk in immediate obedience to the voice of the Father. It comes directly from God. If man gives opportunity, man can take it away. When God is our Source, we will lack no good thing. Awareness of this will keep us in the fear of the Lord. It is often in direct opposition to the systems of this world and commonplace for the friends of God.

   "For You, O Lord, will bless the righteous; With favor You will surround him as *with* a shield" (Psalms 5:12 NKJV).

   For the Lord God *is* a sun and shield; The Lord will give grace and glory; No good *thing* will He withhold from those who walk uprightly. O Lord of hosts, Blessed *is* the man who trusts in You" (Psalms 84:11-12 NKJV).

3. Friendship is not strategic. Friendship is love centered. It stems from honor, gratitude, and a desire to serve. While friendship is often connected to vision, mission, and values, it doesn't end there. True friendship will lay down its life for one another. Those who approach relationship for personal gain are destined to run when trouble comes, but a genuine friend will walk through with you through the valley of the shadow of death. The deepest friendships will ultimately lay down their life for the sake of the other.

   "A friend loves at all times, and a brother is born for adversity" (Proverbs 17:17 NKJV).

When the Bible says, "do not lean on your own understanding," we are to take this seriously and literally. Our hearts are deceitful, our emotions fluctuate, and our limited understanding doesn't see the overall big picture. God knows all, He never lies, and He never changes. Our job is to trust Him. When we face problems and challenges, we can ask the Holy Spirit questions like:

1. How is this situation going to from Christ in me?
2. What does this circumstance mean for my growth and development?
3. How do I partner with you (Holy Spirit) to allow breakthrough to occur?
4. What provision and/or promise is attached to this problem?

When God is our keeper, we can rest. We never have to fear or fret, we can confidently put everything in His hands and trust Him. There's not a situation that can overwhelm us when we practice the Presence of God. It's about responding to God, not acting against people or circumstances. "I will be a Father to you, and you will be my sons and daughters, says the Lord Almighty" (2 Corinthians 6:18 NIV). When we allow Christ to teach us how to be content in all circumstances, we're allowing Him to teach us how strong we really are.

When we encounter things that seem out of whack or a little off, we don't always have to be moved by these things. When we spend time with God and become good receivers of His love, wisdom and understanding, we can love these things. We can learn to appreciate and be grateful for resistance in our lives because it creates clarity. For example, when something is off and we know what God says is true, we can get excited about the clarity that is coming rather than focusing on what's off. The key is to train our focus and deliberately focus on freedom, ease, joy—whatsoever is pure, lovely and praiseworthy and allow that to come forth rather than blocking it's presence. As we maintain our alignment, God can deliver things to us in perfect timing. We don't push, force, or manipulate and insert our will into things, we focus, and trust that God will provide when His time is right.

We're usually much harder on ourselves than everyone else. Growing is giving up the conditional love we've learned and tuned into and operating in our true worthiness. Worthiness feels like putting ourselves in position for and preparing the way for God to show up strong in our lives. We have permission to tune out anything that doesn't resonate with the truth we've discovered. Mastery is where we're able to feel for alignment and find it, know when we're in it and when we're not and maintain our steadiness no matter what. We practice this consistently and deliberately. We allow ourselves to be in alignment with God and all that we are regardless of what anyone says or what's happening. In this understanding is the freedom everyone looks for. It's freedom from resistance that we seek. When we don't understand this, we try to prevent and avoid things. In other words, we want to take action in order to try to make our world as wonderful as we want it to be.

Once we have mastered the understanding that we can control the way we feel because we have the power to focus and then we can practice coming into agreement with God and maintaining steady, chronic alignment and find that through this, only what is wanted is flowing to us. If there is something that is a bit off, we don't freak out, we just take it as an opportunity for a Jesus time out and maintain our grace regardless of it. Unconditional love is alignment regardless of the condition. We have to start with a decision that we want to feel good. If this is our decision then we understand that we can't feel good unless we're really blended with all that we are which causes us to then understand, if we hadn't expanded to more than we can normally maintain than there wouldn't be any new reach. We're designed to go from glory to glory and it requires expansion to do so. We can make peace with the fact that in becoming, we're always reaching beyond our patterns or what's been blocking us to into the more that God has for us.

It's accurate to say that we'll have beliefs that are not up to speed with the whole of who we are. We then are given opportunities to figure out which of those beliefs aren't up to speed with who we are so that we can come back into alignment. Those beliefs are not bad, they support us in furthering our expansion. We can embrace all of our beliefs rather than resist them because our growth matters. If we didn't have the ability to recognize what isn't in alignment, we wouldn't have the ability to recognize what is.

We're not looking for perfection, we're looking for steady things to continue to help us grow and evolve in constant awareness and desire to keep our peace which keeps us moving in the direction of expansion and it's our intent to live joyfully ever after in that way. The neat thing is that if others encounter us and the powerful example we offer, then we are really fulfilling our purpose for being. We weren't born to be an example for them, we were born to be the joyful creators that we are. We can drift quickly the moment we try to insert our influence on others rather than allowing them to expand in their own way and timing. There is no pushing anything away, what we give our attention to, we're calling to us. Our attention to what bothers us only deepens it, but when we laugh and return to love, we're able to perceive things correctly and course correct. As we are determined to not make a big deal over things out of the things that are bothering us, and we add emphasis to the things that are going well, as we make our process be more about steadying our alignment and looking for reasons to feel good, and in doing so meditating and visualizing and focusing we tune ourselves to the frequency of God on a matter. Then we allow Him to control how things come to pass.

Knowing what we don't want, who we aren't, helps us to know who we are and what we do want. It's like flowing downstream and allowing things we're ready for to come to us versus swimming upstream and fighting and resisting and missing things along the way. It's like being an energy connoisseur. We become refined in all things. We get better and better at living aligned and we begin to enjoy the subtleties of our process more. We also begin to feel worthiness as we finally acknowledge that if God is able to inspire us to our unique newness matched with our simple willingness to want to follow-through and understanding of God's Word and truth enough to know that we can become a creative genius on subject after subject. We are the creator of our experience, but God is in on it with us. When we explore and expand beyond our current belief or ability to allow our expansion, God still sees us as He created us to be and holds up His vision knowing that we will find it and not just for the manifestation but the joy in reaching for it.

There are so many wonderful things in the Word of God that teach us what God wants us to have. We can't afford to have an attitude that someone else needs to do it all for us. The happiest people in the world are the most active people. "God make me aware every time I'm thinking bad thoughts." As we begin to pray like that, we'll begin to realize what's in line and what's not with the Word of God. "We demolish arguments and every pretension that sets itself up against the knowledge of God, and we take captive every thought to make it obedient to Christ" (2 Corinthians 10:5). Part of this requires being a diligent student of the Word of God. We can't expect to walk in victory if we're not studying the Word. As we immerse ourselves and apply what we learn, pretty soon we also begin to think in a different way. "Do not conform to the pattern of this world, but be transformed by the renewing of your mind. Then you will be able to test and approve what God's will is—his good, pleasing and perfect will" (Romans 12:2).

Our outer life is our reputation with people, but our inner life is our reputation with God. What's going on inside of you? The inner dimension is a very busy place. The Holy Spirit lives in us and He is traffic light saying stop, go, wait, not yet. There are imaginations in there, opinions, discernment, decisions, attitudes, motives, and purposes. If we want any outer power, we've got to have inner purity. We can easily be led by the Holy Spirit when our heart is pure. Inner turmoil, worry, anxiety, fear, what do people think of me, how do I look…The Bible says instead, "Do not fret because of those who are evil or be envious of those who do wrong" (Psalms 37:1). If we don't learn to calm down inside, we'll never have the impact we're designed to have on the outside. What shows that we're spiritual is when we're put to the test, and we produce fruit.

Where the mind goes, the man follows. We need to think according to the way we want our life to be. We can choose our own thoughts. We're not obligated to think and meditate on whatever lands in our head. Thoughts don't just go away; we have to choose to think on something else. As long as we think that there's nothing that we can do about something than we won't. We can cast down and get rid of wrong thoughts and replace them with the right thoughts. We can think things on purpose.

We renew our mind by reading the Word of God. The only way we can tell a word is wrong is knowing the Word of God. In order to get to the point of knowing and following through on casting down wrong thoughts to choose right ones, you'll have to make the effort and put in the time to study God's Word on a regular basis. "The weapons we fight with are not the weapons of the world. On the contrary, they have divine power to demolish strongholds. We demolish arguments and every pretension that sets itself up against the knowledge of God, and we take captive every thought to make it obedient to Christ" (2 Corinthians 10:4-5).

At the beginning of every year, I'd been accustomed to making a vision board and writing down each desire of my heart in detail and why I desired it. What I found after doing this several times was that I would cling too tightly to these desires and become frustrated when things wouldn't unfold as I'd envisioned and planned. I wanted to be in control of the how when that was God's job. There was no amount of frustration, pushing or hustle that would change that.

I recognized that I needed to start with God before I started running out ahead of Him. I needed to spend more time in His Presence and make meditating on His Word Day and night my habit. As I developed my relationship with God, I decided to start my years differently. Not only would I ask God for a word or theme for each year that I could use as an anchor and a reminder (words like abide, joy, glory have been words I've received as my guides for what to press in for) I would also complete 21 days of prayer and fasting. I would still write down my vision and make it plain, but I would surrender it fully to God acknowledging that He can do exceedingly and abundantly above all I dare ask think or imagine.

This has become a lifestyle practice that I implement anytime I am facing challenging situations, or I need to receive clear direction from God on how to move forward with decision. I've found that when I tune out the world by turning up my connection to God, I actually have more energy, I release anxiety, and I tap into clarity and divine solutions. I expect to hear from God, and I receive wisdom and direction. leave with grand calm your nervous system. I'm also reminded why I need to keep space for God in my life daily. This practice has been truly life-changing and has helped me continue to grow and mature in Christ and experience more of His influence in my life.

To say we're not a disciplined or that it's too hard to change is not true. We have the fruit of self-control. We may not be using it, but we have it. What's in our power to do is in our power not to do. If we can say yes to something, we can say no to it. The choice is ours. The more we discipline ourselves, the more we can control ourselves. For God gave us not a spirit of fear, but of power, love and self-control. Sooner or later, we have to harness our power and focus it into one thing. The first victory we win is over ourselves. We can't do anything great just because we have natural talent, we want to until we first can manage ourselves, we won't be able to manage anything or anyone else. We're all preachers and we say a lot more with our actions than we do with our words.

We can ask the Holy Spirit to help remind us of something or to show us every time we're thinking something we shouldn't be thinking. We can be self-sufficient in Christ sufficiency. Being more than a conqueror is living our lives with a victorious attitude because we already have the victory before we ever had a problem. We don't worry about what will come up tomorrow because we believe we can do whatever we need to do through Christ. Willpower only takes us so far, apart from Him we can do nothing. Many times, God gives us things to do, and we have to take a step of faith before we ever can find out if we can do it or not. "Therefore, as we have opportunity, let us do good to all people, especially to those who belong to the family of believers" (Galatians 6:10).

Our lives are supposed to be salty. We're supposed to make other people thirsty to have a life like ours. If you really want to have victory in your life, you're going to need to learn how to use discipline and self-control on a daily basis. Having it is not the same as using it. We need to toughen up. Getting our lives together requires a level of honesty you can't even imagine. There's nothing easy about realizing you're the one that's been holding yourself back the whole time. When we grow, we build the tenacity we need to be great in the world. If you really want to be a mature, strong and vibrant believer, you will have to through some things that are not very comfortable and learn to go through it, hold your head up high and not whine about it all the time. So often we try to get out of hard things by saying it's just too hard. That is just an excuse and it's a lie. If we want it bad enough, we will find a way. You can say no to anything if you know what the consequences will be if you don't. A lot of our problems are more our own fault than we like to think that they are. Until we take responsibility, nothing can be done about it.

The world should be amazed at believers. We should be the world's heroes, people they can look up to and that can point them in the right direction. If we provide the world with an example of Jesus, they would be encouraged and have hope. Many are called but very few will take responsibility for the call. The work starts with the call, then the sacrifice, then the never giving up, then the going all the way through. A lot of us are called to do really great things, but we have a wrong mindset about what God's asking us to do. Everyone has equal opportunity, all of the power of God available to them but not everybody will do their part. One of the things we cannot delegate is personal responsibility.

We can't do anything apart from God. The key is to always ask God for help. The Word of God has power inherent in it. It's like taking medicine but it's medicine for your soul. You can't change by just trying. You admit your sin, repent, tell God you want to change and study in that area and be diligent. There are unlimited free refills from God.

Activation: Declare your faith! Use the declarations list below to speak over your life.

Remember this: Faith is the evidence of things not seen (see Hebrews 11:1). Our "evidence" for things being true is not our circumstances, but God's promises. We don't deny negative facts in our lives, but we choose to focus on higher reality:

God's truth. Faith indeed comes by hearing (see Romans 10:17); therefore, we choose to speak these powerful truths to build our own faith.

1. I set the course of my life today with my words (James 3:2-5).
2. I declare that I cannot be defeated, discouraged, depressed, or disappointed (Philippians 4:13).
3. I am the head. I have insight. I have wisdom. I have ideas. I have authority (Deuteronomy 28:13, Deuteronomy 8:18, James 1:5-8, Luke 10:19).
4. As I speak God's promises, they come to pass. They stop all attacks, assaults, oppression, and fear from my life (2 Peter 1:2-4, Mark 11:23-24).
5. God is on my side today and therefore I cannot be defeated (Romans 8:37, Psalm 91).
6. I have the wisdom of God today. I will think the right thoughts, say the right words, and make the right decisions in every situation I face (1 Corinthians 2:16).
7. I choose life today. I choose health. I will not be depressed today. I will not be in lack today. I will not be confused today (Deuteronomy 30:19, Nehemiah 8:10, Psalm 103:1-3, 2 Timothy 1:6,7).
8. I expect the best day of my life spiritually, emotionally, relationally, financially in Jesus' Name (Romans 15:13).
9. I speak to this day, and I call you blessed. I declare that I serve a mighty God, who, today, will do exceedingly and abundantly beyond all that I can ask or think (Ephesians 3:20). Thank you, Jesus!
10. I say you are a good God and I eagerly anticipate your goodness today. Thank you, Lord.

This Week: Research and study on fasting and pray for God to guide you in understanding and unleashing the power of it. Fasting is a demonstration of our faith, an intentional pursuit towards a goal or outcome, and a literal spiritual transaction wherein you are prioritizing, taking authority of your life (and flesh), and seeking God with seriousness. When we approach fasting with expectations—something is going to happen as a result.

Here are some benefits and blessings to get you started:

1. Fast in faith fully expecting outcomes and breakthrough (Matthew 7:7-8, Hebrews11:6).
2. Increase discernment of God's will for your life and awareness of Holy Spirit leading (Proverbs 3:5-6, 1 Corinthians 14:33, Romans 8:14).

3. Increase your authority in the spirit, making room for deliverance from difficult strongholds (Matthew 9:29, Luke 4:14).

4. Experience financial protection and maximized success (Malachi 3:10-11, Isaiah 43:16-19, 45:2).

5. Comebacks and come-ups happen (Psalm 118:22-23, 1 Corinthians 1;27).

6. Revelation and understanding of God's Word as He speak to you through the Bible (Isaiah 58:8-9, Psalm 119:130, Hebrews 4:12).

7. Expedited physical and mental healing (Psalm 107:20, 2 Chronicles 7:14, Luke 8:43-48, Luke 8:2).

8. Supernatural protection from enemy attacks (Isaiah 54:17, Jeremiah 33:3, 2 Kings 6:12, Psalm 5:12).

9. Expedited answers to prayers (Psalm 65:2, Jeremiah 33:3, Matthew 7:7).

10. Public rewards for private relationship (Matthew. 6:18, Hebrews 11:6).

A few fasting options:

1. The Daniel Fast:
   - Fruits, vegetables, grains, nuts. No sugar, dairy, sweets, or meats.
   - Pray The Lord's Prayer several times daily, found in Matthew 6:9-13
   - Power Prayers, Praise and Worship—from a place of holiness, purity, and worship taking care to anchor your request or petition in Scripture

2. Fasting from 5AM-5PM:
   - One sensible meal after 5. One meal only.
   - Pray The Lord's Prayer several times daily, found in Matthew 6:9-13
   - Power Prayers, Praise and Worship—from a place of holiness, purity, and worship taking care to anchor your request or petition in Scripture

3. Fruits, vegetables, liquids only. No time restrictions.
   - Pray The Lord's Prayer several times daily, found in Matthew 6:9-13
   - Power Prayers, Praise and Worship—from a place of holiness, purity, and worship taking care to anchor your request or petition in Scripture

4. Liquids only. No time restrictions.
   - Pray The Lord's Prayer several times daily, found in Matthew 6:9-13
   - Power Prayers, Praise and Worship—from a place of holiness, purity, and worship taking care to anchor your request or petition in Scripture

ACTIVATE THE KINGDOM

But the fruit of the Spirit is love, joy, peace, forbearance, kindness, goodness, faithfulness, gentleness and self-control. Against such things there is no law.

—Galatians 5:22-23 NIV

The enemy always fails miserably when he meets a man, or a woman dressed for the occasion. Children of God who are armed and dangerous. Just like the enemy seeks to wreak havoc on everything that matters to us---our emotions, our minds, our families, and our futures, we need to develop a personal strategy to secure our victory. In the book of Ephesians, we find our action plan for putting on our armor:

Finally, be strong in the Lord and in his mighty power. Put on the full armor of God, so that you can take your stand against the devil's schemes. For our struggle is not against flesh and blood, but against the rulers, against the authorities, against the powers of this dark world and against the spiritual forces of evil in the heavenly realms. Therefore put on the full armor of God, so that when the day of evil comes, you may be able to stand your ground, and after you have done everything, to stand. Stand firm then, with the belt of truth buckled around your waist, with the breastplate of righteousness in place, and with your feet fitted with the readiness that comes from the gospel of peace. In addition to all this, take up the shield of faith, with which you can extinguish all the flaming arrows of the evil one. Take the helmet of salvation and the sword of the Spirit, which is the word of God.

And pray in the Spirit on all occasions with all kinds of prayers and requests. With this in mind, be alert and always keep on praying for all the Lord's people. Pray also for me, that whenever I speak, words may be given me so that I will fearlessly make known the mystery of the gospel (Ephesians 6:10-19 NIV).

Sometimes we accept moodiness as a part of life. As long as we're satisfied with that, nothing will ever change. We have to get to the point where we say, "I am tired of the ups and downs, and I must have stability in my life; I don't want to be controlled by my outer circumstances." We can't control a lot, but we can control ourselves through the power of the Holy Spirit. God is not nearly as interested in changing your circumstances as He is in changing us.

Our victory is living victoriously with Christ as we tap into His game-changing reality, our authentic identity, and unveil our strength. We're not wrestling against flesh and blood or man, but against principalities, against powers, against the rulers of darkness of this world and against spiritual wickedness in high places. Often the most difficult person, most pressing problem, and/or most overwhelming circumstance we face is not our real problem. The troubling things in our lives and the things that we perceive with our physical senses are not our real issue. Though we may be wrestling with them verbally, emotionally, financially, even physically, we are wasting precious time and energy that needs to be reserved for the real culprit---the one who is behind the scenes tying to direct the details of some of our most acute difficulties.

Our real enemy, the devil, wants us to ignore the spiritual reality behind the physical one. Because as long as we're focused on what we can see with our physical eyes, he can continue to run rampant underneath the surface. The more we disregard him, the more damage he is free to do. The damage he causes doesn't always look like what we might expect but it's revealed in our strained, damaged relationships, emotional instability, mental fatigue and physical exhaustion. Many of us have experienced feeling pinned down by frustration, anger, unforgiveness, resentment, pride, comparison, insecurity, doubt, discord and fear and the list goes on and on.

Being a child of God doesn't give us immunity from the attacks of the enemy, but it does gives us access to the power of the Father—His power to defend and protect and reverse redeem what's been done. If we want to win the fight, we need to be prepared to flip the script through utilizing the spiritual resources we've been given and have our spiritual eyes opened so that we can see them. We need to take advantage of our heavenly position and benefits package that comes from having every spiritual blessing (see Ephesians 2:6-7, 1:3). Through having eyes that see (vision) and through prayer, we can turn up our fight where we'll actually content for our marriage, believe for our children to be restored, hope for healing, and activate our faith for freedom from addiction. We'll keep asking, seeking and knocking, knowing that surely it will come to pass.

The book of Ephesians is a mix between God's gifts and our responsibilities. We believe and receive first; then we utilize what we've been given. Maturity is God's progressive influence on us. As we apply the truth we've been given, walk righteously and put off the old self (old beliefs and negative behaviors) and put on the new self and new behaviors we're given as seeds from the spirit (see Galatians 5:22-23), we become ready and pure vessels for God's will to flow through. It's on us to live our faith responsibly. Our character development plan is working out our salvation by walking in it (see Philippians 12:2).

One of the things I love about having a master's degree in film production is that it essentially made me a practical psychologist. Because the enemy masters primarily in psychological warfare, I see it as increasing not only my defense but my offense. Through film production I was able to learn about every aspect of film from writing, directing, acting, producing, editing and everything in between. One of the areas that really spoke to me was screenwriting. Whether it was for a feature film or a reality tv show, all of the writing dove into the specifics of character development and understanding what motivate and drives characters, story arcs and the hero's journey, villains and plots twists. It was fascinating to me because it resonated with my life story and journey. I even had a professor say that my life was too melodramatic to be a movie. In other words, my life had so much going on a movie wouldn't capture it.

The feedback stuck, but only because I knew if it were that turbulent, the enemy didn't want a plot twist and God was up to something. As I learned about storytelling, and grew in my understanding, I started developing a practice where I'd play our narratives in my mind. I'd watch different scenarios play out in my mind for how a situation could be resolved so that I could make an informed decision and no react or act impulsively. The great thing about the exercise was that if I'd seen a movie before because I'd lived and learned, I'd get to apply wisdom this time around. Additionally, I could play out worse case scenarios and discover that even if it went that way, I'd be okay, and it would work together for good.

Now I practice this with God. I'll start with questions. What is the enemy trying to do right now? What did God reveal to me/what does God say about this? What is the enemy most afraid of? What does me working this situation from victory look like? After the questions, I let the answers come either through encounters, visualizations, or journaling. Through this I usually receive divine downloads, guidance, or something practical to apply from God's Word. It's incredibly liberating to not have to accept reality as it is and flip the script spiritually and then watch it play out naturally.

What do you want the story of your life to say? God has good plans for us and yet it can seem like when we enter this world, we start out with nothing but blank pages and rolls of film. The story is ours to co-author with God. From when we were first able to make choices, we became responsible for every word on every page we write, every image we capture. We can write a best seller. We can film a family and legacy changing story. We could also just wander and never really create anything meaningful. Wasting the precious gift of life when we were made to rule, and reign would be a tragedy. That's what the enemy wants more of and the story he tried to feed into our minds. We are the lead character in our story and any moment we can decide to become a new, renewed character with a new story. At the end of your life, what is a story that you will love and be proud of?

Communication and having an evolving relationship with God are blessings of a lifetime. It's like breathing; we can't go long without it and it's our life force. Through prayer, are in constant contact with the Creator of the Universe. We get to share our hearts with Him and let Him speak back to us. Through God there is a way for us to be stable. Whoever dwells in the shelter of the Most High will rest in the shadow of the Almighty" (Psalm 91:1 NIV).

God wants to get us to the point where like the Apostle Paul said, he had finally learned to be content to the point where he was not dissatisfied or disturbed no matter what state he was in (see Philippians 4:11-13). Emotional stability isn't just for the people in our lives, but for us because we cannot enjoy our lives if we never know from day to day what we're going to be like.

If we're fighting moodiness and instability in our lives, we need to have some examples around us of what we want to be. If we don't know anyone like that, we start praying for God to connect us with the right people. When we don't see stability, peace or anyone that is spiritually mature, it can seem awkward to embrace or realize we need it. Unhappy people want to make other people unhappy, and if we're not careful we can absorb the wrong influence just by who we hang around. Here are a few practical ways to stabilize our inner life:

1. Get around good people and get good influence in your life. Sometimes we just need to get away from the people that keep us in the pit. You can do it in a way where no one has to get hurt.

2. Spend time in the Word of God. You have to feed on the Word of God and learn to meditate on the Word of God. That means to think about it and roll it over and over in your mind. You can take a certain area of the Scripture like "light" and meditate on the Words about light. It's a matter of forming new habits.

3. Spend time with God. We need to make God first and build our priorities and schedule around Him. It's very important how we get started in the morning so this is a key time. We have the fruit of self-control, and we can develop it. The way anything is developed is through practice.

We have the fruit of the Spirit in us because when Christ comes in us, everything He is and has comes with Him. As a seed, we have what He has. When Christ comes into our lives, the seed of everything God is comes into our spirits. The Bible says the image of Christ is captured in us and we're destined to be molded into the image of Jesus. Our destiny is to be able to get out into the world and act like Jesus. We are to be Christlike in all of our ways. We are holy. Holiness is in our spirit. If we will work with the Holy Spirit and water the seed with the Word of God we will grow and develop little by little.

Images are captured by light. When the light of the world comes into our spirits, the image of Christ is captured in there. For that to be developed it is developed in the dark places of our life, where we have no choice but to be miserable or to start trying to use these great things God has put on the inside of us. Patience for example is a fruit of the Spirit that grows only under trial. Nobody else can develop our fruit of the spirit. Nobody else can develop our peace but us. Nobody can develop our joy but us. The first thing we have to get over is thinking we don't have it. We can control ourselves if you want to.

Nothing changes until we take responsibility for our actions, and we start doing in private for God what we do occasionally to impress people. Until we learn to live before an audience of one and for His glory, not for the admiration of people, then we're not going to consistently do what's right. We might do what's right when we're being watched, but we won't do what's right when we think no one is watching. Then we're living as people pleasers not God pleasers.

Sometimes we use our emotions to get pity and that's the last thing we need because the only way to kill the flesh is to starve it. "Put to death, therefore, whatever belongs to your earthly nature: sexual immorality, impurity, lust, evil desires and greed, which is idolatry" (Colossians 3:5). God isn't into pity. He has real compassion and He's also given us authority. This is something so many are not taught; die to self. We have some wonderful things in our spirit, but we can still have a mess in our soul. We can have the gifts of the spirit and yet operate carnally. We are never going to enjoy stability and spiritual maturity until we learn to do what's right when it feels wrong. Every time we do what's right by a decision of our will using discipline and self-control, to go beyond how we feel, the more painful it is to your flesh, the more spiritually we're growing in that particular moment. We don't have to say everything we feel and we don't have to do everything we feel.

If we want to have freedom, we're going to have to stop letting what other people do control our joy. We start by having those feelings, but no longer giving expression to them. We're no longer going to vent them and we're doing it for God because that's what He asked us to do. Every time we feed something; we keep it alive. We'd stop going around a lot of mountains if we'd close our mouth. We don't change people throwing fits. When something no longer bothers us, we've died to that thing. When we become stable, we can be a witness in an unstable world.

God has picked us out to represent Him. "Therefore, as God's chosen people, holy and dearly loved, clothe yourselves with compassion, kindness, humility, gentleness and patience. Bear with each other and forgive one another if any of you has a grievance against someone. Forgive as the Lord forgave you. And over all these virtues put on love, which binds them all together in perfect unity" (Colossians 3:12-14). At work, the neighborhood, in the church, to our children, to our unsaved relatives. Preaching to people is of no value at all unless we have a witness to go along with it and many times, we're better off to keep our mouths shut and just show them Christ. We have to put on behavior on purpose. We spend time with God to prepare for the stable lifestyle you're determined to go out and live. We think about how we want to behave each day just like what clothes you decide to wear.

We can put on the vision of our future selves that God has revealed to us. We don't have to feel patient to be patient. We don't have to feel confident to be confident. We don't have to feel loving to go love people. As long as we keep following our emotions there will be no stability. The place you can get to is that you can be the same no matter what your circumstances are doing and you don't have to have feelings to act on the Word of God by the power of the Holy Spirit. We are a self-controlled disciplined people and we're not moody. We use our authority to develop our inner life, set our minds, resist the devil, and exercise our faith to call those things that are not as though they are. We are carriers of the Kingdom of God and can activate and release it everywhere we go. We get to co-create with God and craft amazing stories if we choose.

> *Activation:* It's time to fight for what's yours. Develop a prayer strategy using the prayer framework for inspiration. Craft prayers for any area you sense you've been under attack. As you craft your prayers, be authentic, personal, and intentional. The God's Vibes Matter Devotional is a 30-Day Devotional that follows a framework and has prompt to help you cultivate deeper prayer time with God. Visit www.julianapage.com for book details.

> **P**-Praise God. Give gratitude to God for who He is and what He's already done.
> **R**-Repent for any areas where you've been resisting God and turn your heart back to Him.
> **A**-Ask God for your personal and specific requests where you desire to see His hands at work.
> **Y**-Yes! Live as if your prayers have been and all of God's promises have been fulfilled.

> *Examine the Fruit & Check the Armor:* As you're crafting your prayers, also consider what fruit God wants to develop in you in this season? Is your armor fully on and activated? What could use some developing or strengthening?

> *Fruit:* love, joy, peace, forbearance, kindness, goodness, faithfulness, gentleness, and self-control

> *Armor:* Helmet of Salvation (Acts 4:12), Breastplate of Righteousness (2 Corinthians 5:21), Shield of Faith (Hebrews 11:1), Belt of Truth (Proverbs 23:23), Sword of the Spirit (Hebrews 4:12), and Shoes of Peace (Romans 10:15)

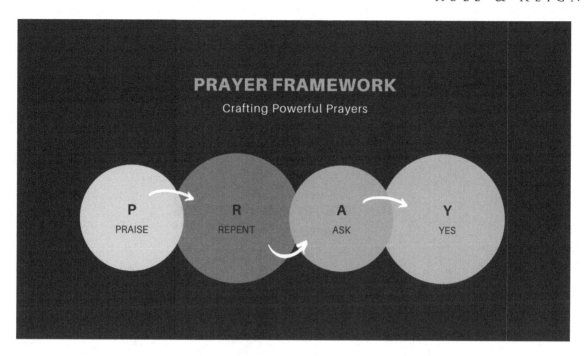

This Week: Any time you find yourself in a low vibe or feeling depressed, shift the momentum. Practice using your tools with this simple formula:

$$PP \rightarrow RR \rightarrow CC \rightarrow DD \rightarrow AA$$

Integrity is keeping promises with ourselves and doing what we say we're going to do when we say we're going to do it. Building integrity momentum comes from being consistent in what we think, say and do. When it comes to faith and activating our authority, it's exercises them when it's easiest not to, over and over. Try this out this week and journal your feedback.

1. **P&P-** Pause and Pray. When you're experiencing an out of alignment moment, pause and pray. Stop what you are doing and go to a place where you can center, breathe, and pray.

2. **R&R-** Rest and Release. We are seated with Christ in heavenly places. Remember to rest your inner life in that truth. Release all your cares to the Lord knowing that He cares for you.

3. **C&C-**Cast down every thought that's exulting itself above the truth. Command and speak God's Word in place of every lie and fiery dart of the enemy attacking your mind.

4. **D&D**-Decree and Declare with your authoritative power what you know to be true and tell the situation to hear the Word of the Lord and come into Kingdom order.

5. **A&A**-Listen for God. What is He saying to you in this moment? Agree and activate His power through receiving it by faith.

BUILD INTEGRITY MOMENTUM
Flipping the Script

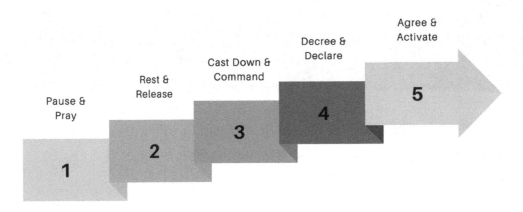

Journal any takeaways from the week:

LEARN TO ENDURE

Consider it pure joy, my brothers and sisters, whenever you face
trials of many kinds, because you know that the testing of your
faith produces perseverance. Let perseverance finish its work so
that you may be mature and complete, not lacking anything.

—James 1:2-4 NIV

There are moments in our lives where things take place, things transpire, and we are never the same after those moments. Our lives are defined by defining moments. Your life may be marked by moments of brokenness, pain or trauma, but as Christ followers, what overshadows every moment is the cross and the resurrection of Jesus. We can point back to the cross every time the devil tries to point his finger in our face and tries to make us believe something inferior.

To endure means to suffer (something painful or difficult) patiently, or to continue to exist without any loss in quality. In other words, to endure is supernatural and the message of the cross and the resurrection breaths healing power into every moment of our lives and enables us to endure. Every disappointment holds divine redemption. Because of the cross all of our pain has a living hope.

The early church was in a defining moment in 1 Peter. They are at a crossroads. They were in the middle of an upheaval where everything they had known had been changed because of Jesus. He opened up a door that they didn't even know existed. They had lived their lives just trying to measure up, trying to be good, trying to be noble, trying to be respected, trying to have everything together, just like so many of us fall into the trap of doing. Then Jesus came with a message of restoration and hope that couldn't be achieved; it could only be received.

Therefore, with minds that are alert and fully sober, set your hope on the grace to be brought to you when Jesus Christ is revealed at his coming. As obedient children, do not conform to the evil desires you had when you lived in ignorance. But just as he who called you is holy, so be holy in all you do; for it is written: "Be holy, because I am holy." Since you call on a Father who judges each person's work impartially, live out your time as foreigners here in reverent fear. For you know that it was not with perishable things such as silver or gold that you were redeemed from the empty way of life handed down to you from your ancestors, but with the precious blood of Christ, a lamb without blemish or defect. He was chosen before the creation of the world, but was revealed in these last times for your sake. Through him you believe in God, who raised him from the dead and glorified him, and so your faith and hope are in God.

Now that you have purified yourselves by obeying the truth so that you have sincere love for each other, love one another deeply, from the heart. For you have been born again, not of perishable seed, but of imperishable, through the living and enduring word of God. For, "All people are like grass, and all their glory is like the flowers of the field; the grass withers and the flowers fall, but the word of the Lord endures forever." And this is the word that was preached to you (1 Peter 1:13-35 NIV).

Jesus being the hinge of hope, opened up a door that had been blocked to provide access to the Presence of God. Now we too have an opportunity to walk into the throne room of heaven. We are Christ followers and the way we live our lives is different than the world around us. We are elect exiles and our behavior hinges on our belief. Our efforts are empty if we're just trying to measure up with what we do. God doesn't want our behavior; He wants our belief. Our belief in Him will intrinsically change our behavior.

It's only when we're changed on the inside that the outwardly actions start to transform. Without salvation there's no reason to obey, without the grace of God, behavior is pointless. "Therefore, rid yourselves of all malice and all deceit, hypocrisy, envy, and slander of every kind. Like newborn babies, crave pure spiritual milk, so that by it you may grow up in your salvation, now that you have tasted that the Lord is good" (1 Peter 2:1-3).

Yes, there's a call on your life, yes there's an invitation for more, yes God will change your actions, but it hinges on the cross. As we look to salvation, we find a new call to action.

"So then, prepare your *hearts and* minds for action! Stay alert and fix your hope firmly on the marvelous grace that is coming to you. For when Jesus Christ is unveiled, *a greater measure of* grace will be released to you. As God's obedient children, never again shape your lives by the desires that you followed when you didn't know better. Instead, shape your lives to become like the Holy One who called you" (1 Peter 1:13-14 TPT). The harvest is plentiful, but the workers are few. We don't need to pray for the harvest, we need to pray that we step into the action that God has prepared for our lives. We've been called to be part of the action.

Peter has some trouble with His behavior, and He has some trouble with His belief. One encounter with the power of the Holy Spirit changed him forever. The one who denied Jesus, was later filled with boldness by the Holy Spirit and as he began to prophecy, he didn't speak looking back at his mistakes, he spoke with power and confidence and authority. His life could have been marked by his denial, instead, the power of the Holy Spirit overshadowed his past behavior and disbelief. It's time to stop looking back at the things that have marked you, hindered you or held you back from the call to action. If you've been wondering if you're called, God knows your name, He created your purpose and if you will obey and step into it, He is waiting to use you.

The Holy Spirit has poured out grace upon us just like He had with the early church. It empowers us. There is an abundance of grace for you and me. Peter's behavior now reflected His belief. It's called holiness. "Instead, shape your lives to become like the Holy One who called you. For Scripture says: "You are to be holy, because I am holy" (1 Peter 1:15-16). Our holiness hinges on His holiness. To follow Jesus is to be holy. It means to walk like Jesus. Why might we need to hold to this word and allow it to shape our behavior?

First of all, it's our influence. As we reflect Jesus, we're able to shine the light of Jesus to a world that is desperate, broken and hurting. Our influence is dictated by our holiness. It's also behind our intention. Our intention should be holy. Our intention should be, God I want to be shaped in your image; I want to reflect you. There is a call to holiness in our day to day. Holiness is allowing the Holy Spirit to show you what Jesus would do. Holiness is surrendering your life to Him. It's the Holy Spirit empowering, comforting, counselling and showing us day by day what the spirit wills for our lives. It all hinges on our belief and what we seek.

Peter tells us not to conform to the evil desires we had when we are living in ignorance. Evil desires aren't just bad things, they could be good things that we try to make God things. We need to be committed to the messiness of allowing the Holy Spirit to transform us from the inside out. We can get so busy trying to live right and trying to live a good life that we can miss out on being spirit led and having an intimate relationship with Jesus.

Peter is calling us to action to be the church. It is not enough for us to be a spectator in what is going on in our world today. Ever since Jesus, we find a new perspective on God.

> Since you call on him as your heavenly Father, the impartial Judge who judges according to each one's works, live each day with holy awe and reverence throughout your time on earth. For you know that your lives were ransomed once and for all from the empty and futile way of life handed down from generation to generation. It was not a ransom payment of silver and gold, which eventually perishes, ¹⁹ but the precious blood of Christ—who like a spotless, unblemished lamb was *sacrificed for us. This was part of God's plan*, for he was chosen and destined for this before the foundation of the earth was laid, but he has been made manifest in these last days for you. It is through him that you now believe in God, who raised him from the dead and glorified him, so that you would fasten your faith and hope in God *alone* (1 Peter 1:17-21).

The way we view God, hinges on our belief and our belief will dictate our behavior and the way that we see God. As we put our trust in Jesus and put our anchor of faith in Him, it gives us a new perspective of the God that we serve. The God that we serve is intimate. He knows every thought before we speak it. He numbers the hairs on our heads. At the same time, He holds the Universe in His hands. God doesn't need us, He wants us. Sometimes we need to think deeper about the price that Jesus paid.

As we think about the price that He paid, we can't help but be in awe of the God we serve. This reverent fear should lead us toward Him, not away from Him. "For through the eternal and living Word of God you have been born again. And this "seed" that he planted within you can never be destroyed but will live *and grow* inside of you forever. For: Human beings are *frail and temporary*, like grass, and the glory of man *fleeting* like blossoms of the field. The grass dries and withers and the flowers fall off, but the Word of the Lord endures forever! And this is the Word that was announced to you" (1 Peter 1:23-25)!

Our new identity is rooted in the imperishable seed of the Word of God. Jesus is the Word made flesh. This behavior that is changing us isn't just a temporary change, but it's been seeded by the imperishable seed of the Word of God. That seed grows as we crave pure spiritual milk; the Word of God. Peter is saying to keep our focus on the future. Keep our focus on where we're going as an elect exile. The only way we can move through this earth with the strength to endure is to let the imperishable seed take root and when we crave that which will nourish and feed our souls. "So abandon every form of evil, deceit, hypocrisy, feelings of jealousy and slander. In the same way that nursing infants cry for milk, you must intensely crave the pure spiritual milk *of God's Word*. For this "milk" will cause you to grow into maturity, fully nourished and strong for life—especially now that you have had a taste of the goodness of Yahweh and have experienced his kindness" (1 Peter 2:1-3).

Fairly early into my journey as a baby believer, I knew that I needed God in my life because I was constantly future-tripping. This probably would technically be considered anxiety, but I was still in the habit and practice of using my newly sanctified imagination in unsanctified ways. I was well-trained since I was a child to anticipate the worst-case scenarios and plan ahead, because unfortunately those were my reality for quite some time. There were many seasons of pain and difficult challenges to endure, that I'd aligned my expectations with believing this was normal and that somehow, I'd just get better at navigating and moving through these. Future-tripping developed as I played out all of the possible scenarios, particularly the worst-case scenarios, so that I would be okay, even if that did happen. The tripping part was because first off, my faith was flowing in the wrong direction and second, the more I thought through and meditated on worst case scenarios, the more I had to do to avoid these. That was no way to live.

Eventually I was led to this verse, "She is clothed with strength and dignity, and she laughs without fear of the future" (Proverbs 31:25 NIV). At first, I found this annoying. I was annoyed at the thought of someone that could laugh without fear of the future. Didn't they know they had to be prepared? See, that was the lie, it was subtle, but that was it. Deep down, I felt unprepared to endure the life I was dealt and the situations that I had to face. As a child, I was without a lot of tools and without having a relationship with God, I was wildly unprotected and unprepared. I began to realize that the reason this woman could laugh without fear of the future was because she knew Who goes before her and who is her rear guard. She knows who holds and maintains her lot (see Psalm 16:5). Could it be that I too was held, covered, supported, protected, provided for, led and guided?

That became my goal, I wanted that word to get down in my spirit that I knew it so deeply that I lived from that place. I needed the future-tripping to cease. I needed my imagination and energy to be freed up to be busy about what who I am here to be versus all I was led to do to protect myself. If I was divinely protected, then focusing on protecting myself no longer had to be my mission. My load would be lighter, and I could walk with my head held high.

I discovered the way to walk this out through prophetic ministry. Many of us are familiar with Jeremiah 29:11, where God tells His people, For I know the plans I have for you," declares the Lord, "plans to prosper you and not to harm you, plans to give you hope and a future." God made this statement to His people while they were in Babylonian captivity for 70 years because they had disobeyed Him. In spite of their behavior, the prophet Jeremiah spoke an encouraging prophetic word to them.

God often uses the prophetic ministry in the same way today, addressing people's potential and not necessarily their present condition. When the gift of prophecy is used to mine the treasure inside of everyone made in the image of God, a major shift begins to take place in him or her. That person no longer sees him or herself enslaved to their present identity or circumstance, but instead is introduced to heaven's perspective. New Testament prophetic ministry speak to the high value and divine potential God has given people. This is the true purpose of prophetic ministry—to be rooted in love, immersed in hope and motivated by faith.

The price that Jesus paid on the Cross determined the value of the people He purchased. God saw something good in us even when we were sinners (see Romans 5:8). We are His treasure, and He is ours. The more I pursued God and the gift of prophecy, the more I looked for gold in the midst of dirt in my life. Prophecy confronts false mindsets and sinful thought patterns with new options, which awakens new realities in the lives of people, often initiating the process of rethinking how we live, love and behave. All were true for me. The more I encountered God's love, the more I was able to laugh without fear of the future and come into alignment with the full potential God created me to be.

Our perspective of God should shape every part of our behavior. We shouldn't look like everyone else. He deserves our awe and wonder and our full focus and attention. Keep entrusting your life to Him and He will keep showing up with exactly what you need. He will carry you through. We have a new grace for others. "Now, because of your obedience to the truth, you have purified your very souls, and this empowers you to be full of love for your fellow believers. So express this sincere love toward one another passionately and with a pure heart" (1 Peter 1:22 TPT).

The gift of salvation has been given to us so that we can love others. We need to strain to love, not strain to judge or to figure out our own ideas or wisdom, we need all our energy to be pointed to loving others around us. Peter tells us to abandon every form of evil, deceit, hypocrisy, feelings of jealousy and slander because all of these things are roadblocks to love and they get in the way of us being the church. Community and the body of Christ isn't just about content but community; that we work out our salvation when we choose to love and get in the messiness of community. "But I have prayed for you, Peter, that you would stay faithful to me no matter what comes. Remember this: after you have turned back to me and have been restored, make it your life mission to strengthen the faith of your brothers" (Luke 22:32).

Make it your life mission to strengthen the faith of your brothers. Jesus spoke over Peter what he would spend the rest of his life doing. Peter's life was marked by surrendering his life to his Savior and being filled with the power of the Spirit. We don't have to be defined by pain and brokenness but by the healer we surrendered our life to. Our life isn't marked by what we did but what He did for us. We put our faith and our trust in Jesus.

Activation: Keep track of your prophetic words. Recording your words and encounters will assist you in developing accountability that builds up your faith. These records may be used as learning and/or teaching tools like films athletes use of their previous fames to improve their abilities. You can record words that you receive live on your phone, you can also release a word and record it as inspired so that you don't forget it. It's best to also transcribe your words so that you can build a track record with God and reference these when your faith needs a boost. Use the image below as a template to transcribe prophetic words. You can write these on index cards with a word on one side and the Scripture that backs it up on the flip side, you can have a prophetic words journal, or you can save these words in a word document—whatever works best for you.

Prophetic Word

Topic:	Date:

Live a full life

Word Given By:	Word Given to:

This Week: God wants to speak to you and through you—and not just for the benefit of everyone else. When we speak to someone, we share our nature with that person by giving of ourselves. We open a flow of relational connection. God wants to speak to you about your life and help bring context to what He's doing in you. If you can interpret God for yourself, hearing Him speak about your circumstances, then you can easily give to others out of that overflow of His heart. When God shares His heart and mind with you about your story, it's one of the most beautiful ways you can experience great growth. Practice hearing from God this week:

Ask the Lord for three personal words, being intentional to ask Him for specific details for each word. Write down these words and details in a journal or safe place. Date them. As the Lord continues to speak to you about each one, add these words to the ones you initially heard. As fulfillment of these words begins to happen, check back on your original words to see how clearly you hear the Lord speaking to you. If you receive a word, ask God what your next step is with that word, then take action on what you hear.

Reminder: It's imperative to have solid community around us as to grow and mature in Christ. We all need spiritual covering and community for accountability and support particularly as we steward prophetic words. If you aren't plugged into a spirit-led and prophetic community, pray for the Lord to lead you to them.

EMBRACE THE NEW THING

Forget the former things; do not dwell on the past. See, I am
doing a new thing! Now it springs up; do you not perceive it? I am
making a way in the wilderness and streams in the wasteland.

—Isaiah 43:18-19 NIV

It's rare that someone is trained to believe in unlimited possibilities. On the contrary, many of us make decisions every day without considering all the available options. For example, the route you take to work every day or the hand you hold your toothbrush in are automatic decisions. They are routine, the outcome is presumed to be known, and we make these decisions without giving them much thought. Consequently, it's easy to go through our days without considering the possibilities, or even being aware that there are other possibilities—until there's a detour because of construction, or for some reason we need to start brushing our teeth with the opposite hand.

While making decision automatically may seem acceptable with little things, if we aren't careful, we can slowly begin to live our lives on autopilot, and this will begin to spill over into other more significant areas as well. In other words, when we have developed the habit of making automatic decisions with all of the little choices, it can become more difficult to stop and reflect on the larger choices when they are presented to us. Only when we've cultivated a practice of awareness can we know if we are making choices based on God's leading, or if we are making choices rooted in limitation. When we aren't able to perceive the new thing that God wants to do in our lives, we end up in the same situations over and over again, making the same choices and then wonder why nothing ever changes. It's only in the realm of the supernatural that true transformation can happen and making conscious choices we know we need to make to evolve despite any fear that arises is very different than allowing fears to dictate our choices. The better we get at communing with God, practicing sensing His Presence and directions, we'll learn more about how to trust Him and build confidence to step out and reclaim our will, authority and freedom of choice.

If we're honest, we depend on miracles for everything—every little detail. We depend on miracles for the love in our hearts, for our patience, for understanding, for our vision, for initiatives, for ideas and for financial resources. Many have also learned that God doesn't tell too much in advance. He tells us what we need to know when we need to know it. If He told us everything in advance, we wouldn't need His magnificent miracles because we would come up with our own plans and then think we don't need Him. God isn't obligated to do anything we say or ask for. In fact, because God is perfect, we are not able to persuade Him to do something that isn't perfect. Unless our will coincides with His, unless it's perfect in His opinion, the answer will be no. God's agenda is different from ours. His agenda is to destroy everything in our hearts that doesn't come from the Holy Spirit. It's in our complete dependency on the Father that we become unlimited.

Limitations are learned. We don't come into the world not knowing what we're supposed to do, those things are learned. It's only when we begin to open up to God and what He has in mind for us, that we notice and are presented with opportunities to go after the new things He's doing. Sometimes we may feel like we're put in situations that we didn't necessarily sign up for. In a story in the gospel of Mark, we see a group of scribes experience this. The scribes showed up with a specific purpose to make sure that the people in Capernaum weren't being taught anything that was wrong. They travelled four days to get there. They were trained in recording the oral tradition surrounding the laws of Moses so that God's people wouldn't forget who they were. Their function was to preserve something that was originally important to the people of God.

> "A few days later, when Jesus again entered Capernaum, the people heard that he had come home. They gathered in such large numbers that there was no room left, not even outside the door, and he preached the word to them. Some men came, bringing to him a paralyzed man, carried by four of them. Since they could not get him to Jesus because of the crowd, they made an opening in the roof above Jesus by digging through it and then lowered the mat the man was lying on. When Jesus saw their faith, he said to the paralyzed man, "Son, your sins are forgiven."

> Now some teachers of the law were sitting there, thinking to themselves, "Why does this fellow talk like that? He's blaspheming! Who can forgive sins but God alone?"

> Immediately Jesus knew in his spirit that this was what they were thinking in their hearts, and he said to them, "Why are you thinking these things? Which is easier: to say to this paralyzed man, 'Your sins are forgiven,' or to say, 'Get up, take your mat and walk'? But I want you to know that the Son of Man has authority on earth to forgive sins." So he said to the man, "I tell you, get up, take your mat and go home" (Mark 2:1-11 NIV).

The scribes were thinking things in their hearts because they'd been in Babylon where God's people had been taken as captives and their customs were different than God's chosen people had ever experienced before. Jesus who is the express image of God to show us what God is really like in the flesh, shows up on the scene to fulfil the Messianic prophecies about Him (to save His people from their sin) and the scribes could not figure out why He was doing what He was doing, it didn't make sense from their point of view and what they had been accustomed to practicing. Have you noticed how easy it is to give up and assume something isn't God's will when we can't immediately see a way in? What this scene demonstrates, is that the oral tradition the scribes we're trained in had become more important than the truth.

Jesus reveals to us that God is a confrontational God. The same God that comforts the downcast confronts the dysfunctional. He loves us too much to leave us in something that is limiting us. If our behavior is never confronted and we can get by just being comfortable, we don't grow. It's the stuff that we would rather not hear that we need to hear. When God begins to deal with us with something that's going to be uncomfortable, we tell God, "Oh no, I'm not ready for that yet." Whatever God wants to deal with us about, there's an anointing at that time for God to deal with us about that thing. Many times, we want to wait for our own timing, and then things can be really challenging. After we're born again, our number one job is to grow up. We need to be stable, not up and down based on circumstances. We also need to be prompt about obeying God because we know that God is smarter than we are and that His way is always best.

The day will come for every one of us when we will stand before God and give an account for our lives. We need to think about that sometimes. It's important what we do with our time and how we treat people. Pursuing God is a sacrifice. It's calling ourselves to a higher level of obedience. Every act of obedience or disobedience is a seed that we sow, that will bring a harvest in our lives. It can bring a harvest that we really like or bring a harvest that we don't like. Very often God puts us in positions in life where we won't like it, and it's not convenient or comfortable and even though we don't understand the purpose, there is a purpose for what God is doing. It usually has something to do with our spiritual growth.

God will shake things up that prevent us from being all He created us to be. God will breakthrough any beliefs that we developed about ourselves, Him, or others. He will see to it that His people are really free. He isn't a conflict avoiding God. Often when we don't experience growth, it's because we won't face the conflict. It's okay to have nice and gentle faith about things in our lives, but there also comes a time when something really matters to God's heart and our hearts that we've got to escalate. God's power doesn't need permission to operate. We can go to Him to get involved and He will step in and confront it.

One of the valuable lessons that I learned through my relationship with God is to let things go when the grace lifts. Sometimes this has been opportunities, volunteer commitments, relationships, churches, dreams, and strategies. A rule that I had made up in my mind was to take God at His Word, and while this is true, that works until God releases a new word or provides new direction. When I challenged my rules, I realized there was an all or nothing approach to how I received some of my directives from God. For example, early on in my faith journey, I was led to serve in a recovery ministry. I didn't know how long I would serve or the full extent of God's plan for me, but after about a year and a half, I started to feel His grace lift. Where once I was clear that God wanted me there, I started to sense He was up to something more but that felt largely unknown. This also conflicted with the messaging of the ministry that reinforced "forever family" and to "keep coming back."

I couldn't deny that through my own inner healing journey with God, that more and more energy was being freed up to do greater things with God and establish His kingdom, but I still didn't have a grid for that, and I sensed the church environment I was in was not matching the hunger that was stirred up in me. I decided to remain faithful for another year and a half, where I didn't take on additional leadership responsibilities, but completed those I was involved in. As I deepened my intimacy with God, I was led to learn more about the prophetic and I quickly discovered this was the more I was after.

After attending a prophetic leadership conference, I felt an anointing to leave the church I was positioned at to explore what church in the local community God wanted to shift me to. Roughly thirteen weekends later, I found myself involved in a new church plant, volunteering, co-leading a life group, taking equipping classes and facilitating prophetic training. What seemed like a long and confusing process initially as the grace lifted, when the time was right, things fell into place quickly and I was accelerated.

Some of my greatest limitation opportunities to shift have been being willing to walk humbly with God and open to how He directs and not to attempt to please people over God. Just because God affirmed something in one season, doesn't mean that it's a fit for every season or even the next season. There are levels to the faith and growth journey with God and we have to be willing to get uncomfortable and go after obedience over everything. I've found that I can be a God pleaser or a people pleaser, but I can't be both. I've noticed this with different leadership opportunities and commitments, that while I'm fully committed and my heart is fully invested, ultimately, I'm responsible to God and not people when it comes to what He's given me to steward. Whenever I've doubted or resisted moving with His grace, things become more difficult and challenging and often lead to the same result (my moving on), with a longer timeline and more frustration.

In the story with the scribes, as the conflict is rising, this shows us the confrontational nature of God. The scribes had turned a gift into a limitation and couldn't perceive the new thing that God was doing. The Sabbath was given to people as a gift, and they turned it into a limit. Similarly, God can give us something as a gift in one season that won't apply to the next season. Our rules for how we expect God to move can restrict the expression that God wants us to bring.

Sometimes what was sent to preserve something can prevent something. Do some rules need to change in your life? What limits are on you or what you think God can do?

The Pharisee in me is who we all have to deal with. If we haven't seen it before we tend to believe it can't be real. "He got up, took his mat and walked out in full view of them all. This amazed everyone and they praised God, saying, "We have never seen anything like this" (Mark 2:12)! The image or imagination isn't matching what's happening. It's breaking the rules. In life we learn lies and become loyal to them and those lies become limits. A lot of times we're waiting on someone else for permission, but we need to get it from within.

> We do, however, speak a message of wisdom among the mature, but not the wisdom of this age or of the rulers of this age, who are coming to nothing. No, we declare God's wisdom, a mystery that has been hidden and that God destined for our glory before time began. None of the rulers of this age understood it, for if they had, they would not have crucified the Lord of glory. However, as it is written: "What no eye has seen, what no ear has heard, and what no human mind has conceived"— the things God has prepared for those who love him—these are the things God has revealed to us by his Spirit. The Spirit searches all things, even the deep things of God (1 Corinthians 2:6-10).

We we're taught how to think about things and if we've never seen it before, it's hard to believe that it can be. "When Jesus saw their faith, he said to the paralyzed man, "Son, your sins are forgiven" (Mark 2:5). Jesus saw their faith, what isn't seen with physical eyes. He saw their faith, not the man on the mat. It's powerful to note, that the right people in our lives can lead us to healing and the wrong people can keep you paralyzed. We can't be loyal to our limitations. When relationships have no more purpose to serve, we need to be brave and bold enough to recognize this and surround ourselves with some new people. When we circle up with people who are stuck in a limitation of what God used to do, it's very hard to believe that all things are possible.

Writer's block, peace block, joy block—the biggest block was in the heart of the scribes who were thinking to themselves. What are the limitations God is calling you to unlearn? "When Jesus saw their faith, he said, "Friend, your sins are forgiven" (Luke 5:20). When his friends had taken him as far as they could, he found a friend that had no limitations. Whatever external limitation there is, God will reveal an internal grace that is greater. The limitation is a gift to show the greatness of God. Jesus can hear thoughts, see faith and a God that can forgive sins.

Put your limitations at the feet of Jesus and position yourself to receive His gift of the new thing. He has all authority. Rise up above what has been holding you and demonstrate the authority of the Word of God in your life. Some things only His Spirit can reveal. When He reveals who you are becoming, you won't be blocked. Ask Holy Spirit what you need to to hone your time and energy in this season. What has He helped prepare, ready and steady you for? Receive His grace and move into the wonderful new.

Activation: Every one of us lives by rules, whether we realize it or not. Most of these rules were just given to us, and we accept them without question. What old rules govern and limit the way you show up in life? What potential new rules are you being guided to live by moving forward? These are your possibilities to draw in the wonderful new in your life. We forget the former things/old rules and ways of being as we get clear on, embrace, and act out the new ways of being. Write out a list or draw the diagram in a journal and fill in the circles.

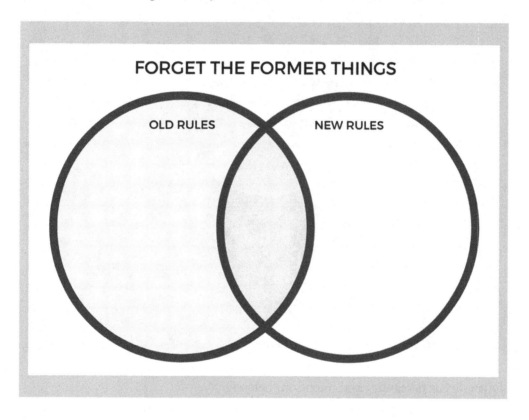

FORGET THE FORMER THINGS

OLD RULES   NEW RULES

This Week: Based on what God's Word/Truth says, what do you need to believe about God, yourself or aspects of life in general to perceive the new thing God wants to do in and through you? All that you can control is the moment that you're in, not the past, and not the future. Brining yourself to a state of awareness and being present in the moment takes practices but is it essential to creating new things.

Think of yourself like a jar full of God potential energy. If you're worried and anxious, some of that energy leaks out of the jar. At the same time, as you connect with God, grow in awareness of His promises and Truth and receive divine revelation and inspiration, you are present and not only have a full jar, but it starts to overflow. You're meant to live from a place of overflow. This week, think about what's in your jar—is it the Promises of God, belief, and anticipation of the wonderful new and you show up in the moment or is it a to-do list, what's not working, what bad things might happen and moodiness? Ask God to reveal what adjustments you can make to shift out of fear and back into the awareness of His love.

Journal your takeaways and intentions below:

PRACTICE RADICAL LOVE

But we all, with unveiled face, beholding as in a mirror the
glory of the Lord, are being transformed into the same image
from glory to glory, just as by the Spirit of the Lord.

—2 Corinthians 3:18-19 KJV

Jesus invites us into a relationship with Him, not a religious reform program. He showed up in the midst of our brokenness with compassion and healing, shocking everyone by how fearless He was about being radical with His love with sinners. He didn't create distance with broken people; He created connection. His entire mission was to finally remove sin—the source of all relational disconnection—through the cross. Jesus solved the sin problem for good—not only ours but the whole world's (see John 2:1-2). It doesn't matter who has or has not "prayed the prayer." Sin has been handled, and everyone has access to the Father.

God knew exactly what He was getting into when He went into the people business. He has the most blindingly brilliant plan for separating us from our mess every time, no matter how big; the cross. By solving the sin problem, Jesus created a safe place—the safest place in the world for us to be loved, known, accepted and forgiven. He did give us one big requirement if we want to live and flourish in this safe place of relationship with Him: that we love one another as He has loved us. As John wrote, "My dear children, let's not just talk about love; let's practice real love. This is the only way we'll know we're living truly, living in God's reality" (1 John 3:18-19 MSG). Our spiritual calling is nothing less than to love and to be loved by God and people. Our spiritual training and growth can only occur in the context of relationship.

The whole nature of relationship is that we can't control it. All we can control is our free choice to love others and receive their love. When we make this choice, freedom grows, and fear goes. It will require that we grow up and become powerful. The more powerful we become, the more we will be able to hold on to our connection with people and help them as they work through their truth and clean up their mess—just like Jesus does. No matter what miraculous things God is doing around us and through us, we must never lose sight of this priority. Do you want Jesus to know you? Do you want to know Him? Then love Him and love others. The Bible couldn't be clearer about this: "But if anyone loves God, this one is known by Him. Beloved, let us love one another, for love is of God; and everyone who loves is born of God and knows God. He who does not love does not know God, for God is love" (1 Corinthians 8-3, 1 John 4:7-8,

NKJV). Just imagine what would happen if we started walking around with hearts three times as powerful and love as anyone else around us. People might actually start believing that God is real. We'll need big hearts to mature into powerful people who know how-to walk-in freedom, practice intimacy and vulnerability, clean up our messes, and invite people around us to becomes powerful, free lovers.

The degree to which we have changed is evidence of what has been changed or converted in us. Have you been converted? After God created the world, He planted a garden "and put [Adam] in the garden of Eden to tend and keep it" (Genesis 2:15). This is a picture of each of our lives. God has given all of us a garden to tend. He plants trees in it and sends the sun and rain to make them grow. But we are the ones who have the responsibility to care for the trees and the right to enjoy their fruit. No one else has that responsibility. Only in being diligent in managing what is ours will we reap a harvest that will nourish us and give us something good to offer others. If we don't take care of ourselves and do our work, we won't be able to care for anyone else.

The only reason the enemy attacks us is because he sees our potential. He knows the things that God wants to give us, and he desires to work his three-part agenda to kill, steal and destroy these things. If we truly want to be loving and unselfish, we will take the time and effort to get our garden producing the best fruit possible so we can offer something valuable to others. We will invest in learning all there is to now about the garden God has given us—from our physical, emotional, mental, and spiritual health to our education, talents, gifts, callings, finances, relationships and move—and how to make it flourish. God prayed for us because He has a plan for us. He wants to do a work of grace in our lives that changes our hearts. The more we respect the value of our own lives by cultivating the garden, the more we will change the atmospheres around us with the kingdom.

Often, when we stop thinking we're ready for stuff we're not ready for, humble ourselves, discover our own wretchedness, and walk away from the idols of positions and titles, that's when God will call us and use us like we've never been used before. Our life with Jesus is designed to be a life of impact and substance. We've never been called to the shallow like the world suggest. We're never satisfied with shallow things because something in us can distinguish and discern what is low-level. People of God, people of relevance and destiny, talk about ideas, purpose, vision, and the Kingdom, the deep things. We're built for deep waters.

Until we hunger and thirst to be better men and women, husbands and wives, witnesses, and leaders, we won't change. God isn't our God to be our manager or promoter, we're here to see His greatness and promote that. His greatness is humbling. Sometimes what we need is to pray that we'll have such an encounter with God that we won't define our Christianity by what church we go to or our title but the changes we've experienced because we've been converted. How are you different? God won't do it all for us. We've got to do better. We all have something to bring to Jesus. The way we think, act, our focus, discipline, insecurities, ulterior motives—we need a metamorphosis to begin. We need to let the Holy Spirit come into our heart and help us do deep inner work.

When I was finally ready to start cleaning up my mess and tending to my garden, I fully surrendered my life to Christ. I didn't know the Father's love and I needed it desperately to heal my heart and to help me show up differently in the world. I'd been struggling with a lot of anxiety about the future, I'd build so many walls to protect myself, I'd blocked myself from receiving a lot of good things and I was struggling to survive when I knew I'd been called to thrive.

After pouring my heart out to God, the very next day, I woke up without a desire to give into a food addiction. In its place I was given strategies to start walking out a healthy relationship with my body and eating habits. I was also given energy to level-up all of my lifestyle habits from my sleeping routine, workouts and mental health. I was led to books, sermons and even therapists, coaches and mentors that could support and guide me as I grew in my relationship with God and my own self-love.

What fascinated me, was that thing I'd struggled with for years, started falling off my life and I was working with greater ease to build a new and firm foundation in my life. As I spent time with God, I also gained the ability to cry again as He cleansed and repaired my heart. I started being drawn to more knowledge about the kingdom and how to live as a new creature, and I found myself stepping not only into love, but more freedom. I no longer resisted my growth journey, I fully prioritized it and invested in it because my life depended upon it.

The Gospel of Luke shares a transformative moment in the life of Jesus and His disciples. Transitions can be uncomfortable because they are so nebulous and uncertain. They're an in between spot where we can't really draw from where we've been, and we can't really receive the benefit of where we're going. We're just in the process of change. Jesus did not give in to people who didn't stand by Him in His trials.

> They began to question among themselves which of them it might be who would do this. A dispute also arose among them as to which of them was considered to be greatest. Jesus said to them, "The kings of the Gentiles lord it over them; and those who exercise authority over them call themselves Benefactors. But you are not to be like that. Instead, the greatest among you should be like the youngest, and the one who rules like the one who serves. For who is greater, the one who is at the table or the one who serves? Is it not the one who is at the table? But I am among you as one who serves. You are those who have stood by me in my trials. And I confer on you a kingdom, just as my Father conferred one on me, so that

you may eat and drink at my table in my kingdom and sit on thrones, judging the twelve tribes of Israel.

"Simon, Simon, Satan has asked to sift all of you as wheat. But I have prayed for you, Simon, that your faith may not fail. And when you have turned back, strengthen your brothers." But he replied, "Lord, I am ready to go with you to prison and to death." Jesus answered, "I tell you, Peter, before the rooster crows today, you will deny three times that you know me." Then Jesus asked them, "When I sent you without purse, bag or sandals, did you lack anything?" "Nothing," they answered. He said to them, "But now if you have a purse, take it, and also a bag; and if you don't have a sword, sell your cloak and buy one" (Luke 22:23-36 NIV).

Conversion doesn't necessarily mean faith, but anything that changes fundamentally from one thing into another. Jesus confronted His disciples and each one is examining himself for the possibility that it could be possible that Jesus was talking about him. No one escapes that examination that we could in some way be betrayers of Jesus. The disciples go from asking "Lord is it I to who's going to reign with you" to "Am I a devil or am I going to sit on the right or the left?" They're jockeying for a place. They'd been listening to Jesus preach but they hadn't been hearing Jesus preach and in the back of their minds, they can't figure out how everything fits together.

Jesus didn't come to overthrow the old kingdom but to bring a new one. The disciples saw the crown, but they didn't see the cross. As we see in this story, God isn't afraid to set it off in the middle of chaos. What He needed to do was allow the disciples to have the ultimate rejection. Some people you can't help until they hit rock bottom. It's amazing that they could walk with Him that long and still not get Him. They we're being challenged to evaluate several things:

- Position – The disciples were so fleshly that they were worrying about being recognized as important. In God's Kingdom, the way up is down. The lower we go in the Kingdom the higher God will exalt us. God defines greatness by humility. Unless we become like little children you will not inherit the Kingdom (Mat. 18:3). The better we are at serving, the higher He'll raise us.

- Perspective – We always talk out of our perspectives, our life experiences, and points of view. What we conclude whether it's the right or not, is the sum of our perspectives and experiences. Our opinions are concocted out of our experiences. Jesus's disciples had an earthly perspective, and His perspective was heaven's. What we see in this story is the wrestling of perspectives.

- Potential – How many times have you told God you were ready? How do you know that you're ready? Often, we have the potentials of being ready but not the preparation of being ready. Wanting it doesn't make us ready for it. The pain of potential is to know that we have the potential but we're not ready for it. We've got the raw skills to be great, but all of the talent put together has not gotten us there and we're bitter because potential has given us pain. The people with the greatest potential live up under the greatest attack. When we've been converted-same man or woman but converted. The goal is the conversion of the soul. When we are converted our potentials will be utilized. God can't fully use us just because you follow Him. When were converted, we're hungry for the Word and for truth, and we apply it to grow in our connection with God and to work out our potential.

- Provision – The stronger we get; the less God does for us. The older children get, the less we have to do. God won't do baby food miracles for grown up believers. He won't do what He used to do. He'll require more of us. We'll have to invest in ourselves. We can't just pray and wait on Him to do it. He'll still provide but He'll provide through us and not just to us. He will require our participation in our provision in order to take us where He's going to take us. He won't just open doors. We'll have to be intentional.

- Promise – We'll know we're converted by the affect we have on other people. The way our presence strengthens people is a sign we're ready. It's our "bretheren" that will show us we're converted. We'll have an effect on them that we didn't before. We'll have impact not just effort.

Is there something about your life that doesn't say conversion? Is there fruit? Is there evidence? What do you need to re-examine? When we enter into relationship with Christ, the Bible tells us that we become new creations (see 2 Corinthians 5:17). Old things have passed away, and we are given an opportunity for a new beginning. We become new spiritual clay for the Holy Spirit to work with. He shapes us into beautiful vessels, perfectly designed for the great purposes He has for our lives.

Conversion costs us something. We can't just sit, hope and wish, we have to take practical actions to go after whatever it is. It doesn't just happen through divine osmosis and it's not always about what we want, what we feel and what makes us happy.

Consider:
What are you going to do?
What are you going to be better at?
What will be your real evidence that you've been with Jesus and that He's been with you?

Between you and God, what are you giving Him? Is it:

- Murmuring and complaining
- People-pleasing
- Second-guessing
- Doubt and guilt
- Shame and fear of wrong/bad choices
- Weak boundaries and being casual

Or is it:

- Quality time
- Devotion and worship
- Faith and trust
- Guarding heart, words, actions, thoughts
- Holding tongue/keeping mouth shut
- Speaking life, encouragement, and love (what transforms things)
- Courage and boldness

Think what could have happened but didn't because God prayed for you. God is never going to deal with you without giving you the ability to go all the way through to victory, but you've got to believe it. Our secrets will make you sick. No matter what has happened or is going on right now, it doesn't have the power to keep you from having a great life if you will have a positive vision for the future.

Some of the old ways we've done things are dead. Step up into a new level of responsibility and stop putting things off until another more convenient time. The only way out is through. We need to pray, but a lot of times when we pray, God shows us something to do. The Bible says to look at the aunt who works hard and does what's right without an overseer. Are you someone who will do what is right when no one is looking?

Everybody wants to do something for God, but how many are willing to do the years of preparation? It's easy to want something, but there's always a lot of hard work and changes in our lives that go with it. Growing with God is the best opportunity that anyone could have. If we think that there's something that God wants us to do, we can't let anything stand in our way. Rather than running away from it, we run to it. If we're going to move with God we're going to have to learn to move by instinct.

Activation: What are you requesting that God help you to do in this season? What are you going to offer God? Use the image below to guide a conversation and encounter with God.

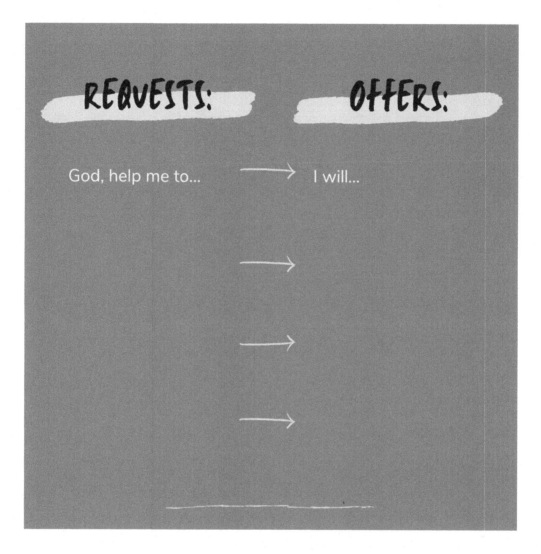

This Week: Write a letter from your future, big hearted self to your current self. How does God want to speak through the future version of you, to who you are right now to encourage your heart?

A LETTER FROM MY FUTURE SELF

Dear Current Self,

CONCLUSION

Rule & Reign in Life

And God blessed them. And God said to them, "Be fruitful and multiply and fill the earth and subdue it and have dominion over the fish of the sea and over the birds of the heavens and over every living thing that moves on the earth.

—Genesis 1:28 NIV

*I*t is your season. It's your season for growth, breakthrough and the greater. Now is the time where you'll see your faith go to work for you. You will see the Lord's favor come upon you because God always rewards those who diligently seek Him. What you're dreaming about, what you're believing God for, the thing that He has spoken to you about you (you know what that is), the time has come for that to exit your mind and manifest on earth. Commit these things to paper. If God can't trust you to take that simple step, what makes Him think that you're the one to steward the blessing or occupy the territory?

As you prepare for your season, here are some verses and truth to get rooted and grounded in.

1. Begin your process. Don't delay, tarry, procrastinate or put it off. Go and make it plain. "**Eternal One** *(to Habakkuk)*: Write down this vision. Write it clearly on tablets, so that anyone who reads it may run. For the vision points ahead to a time I have appointed; it testifies regarding the end, and it will not lie. Even if there is a delay, wait for it. It is coming and will come without delay" (Habakkuk 2:2-3 VOICE). Writing the vision is your creative expression. The goal of getting clear is to accelerate you into the manifestation of your vision and God's promise for your life.

2. Make up your mind that you're creative. God is a creator. Everything you see in this world, was made by God (not wickedness and wicked things). We are to fix our mind on all of His wonders. "I remember the glorious miracles of days gone by, and I often think of all the wonders of old" (Psalm 143:5 TPT). We also need to remember just how big and powerful God is. "Who is it that travels back and forth from the heavenly realm to the earth? Who controls the wind as it blows and holds it in his fists? Who tucks the rain into the cloak of his clouds? Who stretches out the skyline from one vista to the other?

What is his name? And what is the name of his Son? Who can tell me" (Proverbs 30:4)? God is creative and powerful, so are you.

3. Take the limits off. You haven't seen all that you are capable of yet. You have gotten a glimpse of your destiny, but you haven't seen anything yet. God is stretching you right now. You're made in His image, and you carry His creative power. The season you're getting ready to enter is going to blow your mind. God is going to do things in your life and through your life that are bigger than you dreamed. That's why your preparation is so important. Every animal of field and forest belongs to me, the Creator. I know every movement of the birds in the sky, and every animal of the field is in my thoughts. The entire world and everything it contains is mine" (Psalm 50:11). God wants to do big things in your life. He wants to do big things in the earth through your life. You are here for such a time as this. You are anointed for this generation. You are anointed for this nation. God is not finished in your life yet. There is still so much inside of you. There will be acceleration that comes on your life taking you from where you are to what's next. He wants to shift you and lead you into the greater. It begins for many of you by clarifying your vision and taking the limits off it.

4. There are assignments just for you. "For by grace you have been saved by faith. Nothing you did could ever earn this salvation, for it was the love gift from God that brought us to Christ! So no one will ever be able to boast, for salvation is never a reward for good works or human striving. We have become his poetry, a re-created people that will fulfill the destiny he has given each of us, for we are joined to Jesus, the Anointed One. Even before we were born, God planned in advance *our destiny* and the good works we would do *to fulfill it*" (Ephesians 2:8-10)! You were created for things He created for you to do even before you were born. There are assignments that are just for you. There are opportunities that are only for you. There is inheritance that is just for you. That is the size and the scope of your destiny.

5. Sit in your prayer chair. Go into your Jesus space, go into your prayer closet and seek, ask. There are some things that will not be released to you unless you ask. There are some things the Lord will not even reveal to you unless you take the initiative to knock. "Ask, and the gift is yours. Seek, and you'll discover. Knock, and the door will be opened for you" (Matthew 7:7). "**Eternal One:** Call to Me, and I will answer you. I will tell you of great things, things beyond what you can imagine, things you could never have known" (Jeremiah 33:3 VOICE). You are getting ready to knock, ask and to seek; what is the Lord's will for you in this season of your life? Because you will take the initiative to call

to Him and ask Him to show you great and mighty things, which you knowest not, a reward is going to be that God is going to answer you. The Lord will answer you and you will know that you know, with no confusion His will (see 1 Corinthians 14:33).

6. Stay steady and persistent. Your "seek" will be as music to His ears. He's been waiting on you. He's been waiting on you to ask and seek confirmation. It takes a certain kind of person to take the initiative to seek. Many people are hoping things will just show up; that they don't have to do anything at all. It takes a certain kind of person to begin to seek; to hit their knees and seek the Lord. You won't quit until you get your confirmation. That's someone the Lord knows He can use. You've already demonstrated that you have initiative and persistence. You are not one who's just going to pursue what seems good to you. You're not just going to be wise in your own eyes. You know there is One who is far wiser that you need to consult. You want Him to order your steps. You don't want to call your best shot and hope it works out. You know you've already done that. Too many times for some of you. The result for some is that you spend time, seasons and maybe even years in the wrong relationships, at the wrong company, in the wrong place, investing into the wrong projects and people.

7. Increase your faith. Some people have a hard time getting into agreement with the vision or the instruction God gives because they don't have God-size faith. If you're talking to someone who isn't firmly rooted in the Word, (they have their own seek going on) they have a firm relationship with Jesus and they too are chasing the destiny for their lives, and they haven't slowed down. Some people aren't tight with God the way you know God. So when you begin talking about the Lord, and the vision He gave you and what you believe your destiny is, some people can't see it and they're going to try to apply the wisdom of the world to the dream that God gave you. God gives you God-size dreams and visions and it will seem like foolishness to people who are in the world. It will seem so crazy and so far out, impractical and unrealistic. It usually is. If it was practical and realistic, you could do it yourself. Why would you need God? That's not how you bring forth God-size destiny. God needs us to step out of the boat and that's when we start losing people. It seems unwise, unrealistic, and dangerous. Not to the Lord who made the water. He designed this planted and all of life on it. He's challenging some people to stop questioning the size of the vision that He gave you. One way you know a vision is from Him is when it's huge and you don't know how you're going to do it.

8. Develop your character. God cannot open doors for you and usher you into realms that your character cannot sustain. It's not so much that you won't be able to walk through

the door, but you need to be able to occupy the territory that God gives you access to. You need to be able to sustain yourself in the blessing that the Lord releases to you so stop trying to skip steps. Stop trying to access something too soon. If this next dimension was made available to you too soon, and you are not ready, it would feel like more of a curse than a blessing. Your anointing can take you there, but you need the character to sustain you there. The mantle that you carry and that you wear that can take you there, but you need the spiritual foundation to sustain you there. No more trying to skip steps. There is acceleration to be had and some will go so quickly that it will blow your mind. God is going to do a quick work that's why preparation is so key. "Beloved friends, what should be our proper response to God's marvelous mercies? To surrender yourselves to God to be his sacred, living sacrifices. And live in holiness, experiencing all that delights his heart. For this becomes your genuine expression of worship. Stop imitating the ideals and opinions of the culture around you but be inwardly transformed by the Holy Spirit through a total reformation of how you think. This will empower you to discern God's will as you live a beautiful life, satisfying and perfect in his eyes" (Romans 12:1-2 TPT). There are levels to your destiny, and it never ends. The Lord always has more for you. He always has higher for you.

9. It doesn't have to make sense to you. Vision is translated to mean prophetic revelation. This prophetic revelation that you are going to seek and obtain from the Lord, is crucial. When the Lord nails it down for you, you better be ready. You're going to feel like someone lit a firecracker on the inside of you and you won't be able to pursue quickly enough. That's the difference in a prophetic vision. That's the impact that it can have on your life. When you ask the Lord with sincerity in your heart and spirit, and He knows that you mean business and you are truly seeking understanding and revelation, it will come quickly. This is no time to make moves based on your past experience or even the advice of someone who might mean well, but they're not God. They don't know all the details that the Lord knows. They don't know what's coming next for you. Seek the Lord and let Him order your steps. "When there is no clear prophetic vision, people quickly wander astray. But when you follow the revelation of the Word, heaven's bliss fills your soul" (Proverbs 29:18 TPT). It doesn't have to make sense to you because God works on a level and at a size that is unnatural to human people. If you don't commit without wavering, it is a given that the cares of life or life in general will come to try to steal your vision and that too is a way that the enemy will try to kill, steal, and destroy.

10. Get the doubt out. No, "I hope so" or "we'll see." Whatever you pray for, believe if you want to receive. There's nothing that's impossible for God. You're not going to allow any

unforgiveness to block you. Just forgive them all. You've made up your mind that you're not going to let any of it block you. "This is the reason I urge you to boldly believe for whatever you ask for in prayer—be convinced that you have received it and it will be yours. And whenever you stand praying, if you find that you carry something in your heart against another person, release him and forgive him so that your Father in heaven will also release you and forgive you of your faults" (Mark 11:24-25). When it's your season, things change, and they start with you.

People might say there is no guidebook for life, but the Word of God is the highest authority on the planet. "Let us hold unswervingly to the hope we profess, for he who promised is faithful" (Hebrews 10:23 NIV). When we know, believe, declare and stand on the Word, something has to happen. If God said it, He will do it. " Let us not become weary in doing good, for at the proper time we will reap a harvest if we do not give up" (Galatians 6:9).

What are you saying? Don't let the devil catch you slipping. Don't allow your faith, confession or obedience (or lack of) give him anything to work with or accuse you of. Stand on the promises of God and position yourself to be blessed. "So be careful to do what the Lord your God has commanded you; do not turn aside to the right or to the left. Walk in obedience to all that the Lord your God has commanded you, so that you may live and prosper and prolong your days in the land that you will possess" (Deuteronomy 5:32-33).

Your life is not like people who don't serve God. You are in covenant relationship with the Lord and God takes care of His own. Be willing to grow. "Therefore, I urge you, brothers and sisters, in view of God's mercy, to offer your bodies as a living sacrifice, holy and pleasing to God—this is your true and proper worship. Do not conform to the pattern of this world, but be transformed by the renewing of your mind. Then you will be able to test and approve what God's will is—his good, pleasing and perfect will" (Romans 12:1-2).

This happens by studying and reading the Word. As you read God's Word, you learn who God is, His character, His standard, and you learn who you are and what God asks of you and what He promises. As you position yourself to be blessed, to really immerse yourself in the word, prayer, praise, worship, and spending time with Jesus unlike ever before, you can fully expect to see the Presence of God and the hand of God in your life like never before. You can also expect transformation to begin to happen in your life. It doesn't matter how long you've been following Jesus, how young or how old you are, there's always more in God.

Transformation is a key that unlocks revelation to your destiny. As you continue to grow in this wonderful faith walk with the Lord and continue to transform and be strengthened and stretched and increase, God is going to reveal things to you. He's going to start talking to you about what comes next for you—the good, acceptable and perfect will of God. There are levels to your destiny. God has another level for you. If you're willing to grow by being transformed by the renewing of your mind, you'll position yourself to be blessed.

> My son, do not forget my teaching, but keep my commands in your heart, for they will prolong your life many years and bring you peace and prosperity. Let love and faithfulness never leave you; bind them around your neck, write them on the tablet of your heart. Then you will win favor and a good name in the sight of God and man. Trust in the Lord with all your heart and lean not on your own understanding; in all your ways submit to him, and he will make your paths straight. Do not be wise in your own eyes; fear the Lord and shun evil. This will bring health to your body and nourishment to your bones. Honor the Lord with your wealth, with the firstfruits of all your crops; then your barns will be filled to overflowing, and your vats will brim over with new wine (Proverbs 3:1-10).

The power of obedience. Your truth, your direction, your understanding is found in the Word of God. If there is anything you ever see in the world or hear on tv or the news that contradicts the Word, throw out the lie and stay with the Word of God. When you declare the Word of God over a situation, eventually you'll begin to see that situation change because it must come into alignment with the Word of God.

When you prioritize the Word, the result will be that you will find favor in the sight of God and man. In all your ways acknowledge Him. Give Him all the glory. You need to be in good condition for Him to give all that He wants to give and do for you. He wants you to have excellent health. Be strong and courageous as you go forth into your future and the Lord shifts you into a brand-new season. The battle is the Lord's. You have no idea what God will release to you simply because you have bold and audacious faith. That tells Him you trust that He can do it. "Therefore I tell you, whatever you ask for in prayer, believe that you have received it, and it will be yours" (Mark 11:24). Doubt is a poison to your faith. Have the childlike faith that He will come through for you.

What's most important to your existence is that you know you're fully loved. Relationship with God is not dependent on how much we love God, but on how much He loves us. Jesus represents that God did what was necessary to get to you. The ultimate expression of God's love was a sacrifice. You can only know what you're passionate about by what you're willing to sacrifice for. Insanity is searching for love and running from God. Believe that God is for you and that He set you free to be who you were created to be. Decide He can be trusted. God will meet you where you are and your life will change if you're willing to cross the line of faith.

Dare to believe and dream big. It's time for you to stir up your faith and believe God for something big in your life. Write down your petitions and what you're believing for and what you hear the Lord say. Find promises in the Bible that you're believing to come to pass for you. Bring it to the Lord and believe that you will receive. God is doing mighty things in our midst, and you'll have a praise report sooner than you think. He's got something good for you and we give Him glory in advance. There's more for you that's why you have this manual. May you know the beauty and the joy of the God connection and experience and release His love like never before.

RESOURCES

To learn more about coaching, consulting, mentorship programs and courses or to invite Juliana Page to speak, visit: www.julianapage.com

PODCAST

The Spirit-Filled Real Talk Podcast is just that—real talk that's spirit-filled and backed with the Word of God. Tune in wherever you get your podcasts for a healthy dose of soul fitness with your go-to gal for spirit-led business and personal development! Listen weekly for practical wisdom and encouragement to equip and empower you mentally, emotionally and spiritually.

BOOKS

God's Vibes Matter: Reclaiming Your Spiritual Authority

In God's Vibes Matter: Reclaiming Your Spiritual Authority, author Juliana Page shows how to have a heart fully surrendered to the transformative power of God's Spirit. Juliana shares lessons about the everyday miracles that illuminate God's Spirit, and she shows how these lessons, along with insightful journal prompts, will inspire Spirit seekers to look deeper into their own stories, empowering them to prosper through Spirit-led living.

God's Vibes Matter Co-Laboring with God

In God's Vibes Matter: Co-laboring with God, author Juliana Page shows how to identify when we are living a life apart from God - a life in which he is not consistently present in our thoughts and words. Thankfully, God wired our thoughts and words to have power so we'd be equipped to overcome every obstacle. However, without consistent exposure to the ultimate power source - our light source -our hearts are not hooked up to the provision they need.

God's Vibes Matter Devotional

This 30-day daily devotional is an invitation and a challenge that will change your life! In the devotional, Juliana Page invites believers on a 30-day journey of divine encounters. Juliana provides a prayer framework for followers of Christ to reshape their thinking and delight in the inspiration, hope, and encouragement of encountering God's presence.

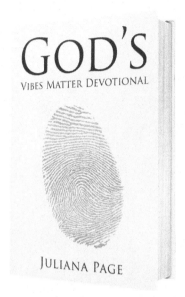

Printed in the United States
by Baker & Taylor Publisher Services